The Bear Dogs of Katahdin

THE BEAR DOGS OF KATAHDIN

And Other Recollections of a

Baxter State Park Ranger

Steve Tetreault

To order additional copies of this book, contact:
Xlibris Corporation
1-888-795-4274
www.Xlibris.com
Orders@Xlibris.com
44688

CONTENTS

FOREWORD

A book such as this is never written alone. It is really a book of memories. As I delved into my memory to recall the following stories, I was able to fondly remember many people. Greg Hamer and Scott Fisher actually came up with the idea of putting our ranger stories down on paper. My wife, Pat, Scott and I were visiting Greg at Russell Pond in September 2005. Greg is still a Baxter ranger whereas Scott and I have had to turn to other employment over the years. But whenever the three of us get together, it's easy to reminisce about our time together at Baxter Park. If I'd only had a tape recorder that night in September 2005. If it weren't for my mom and dad, Fran and Joe Tetreault, I would never have been able to attend Unity College and earn my ranger degree. Retired Unity College Professor, Mr. Donald Mortland graciously agreed to edit the stories, but any mistakes are mine alone. My daughters, Amie and Emily, were among the first to read the stories and encourage me to write more of them. Thanks to all of you.

CHAPTER 1

IT HAD TO START SOMEWHERE

I had decided with conviction to become a park ranger when I grew up. I was only seven years old. Why had I so firmly decided my life's course at such a young age? I have no idea. All I knew was that I wanted to be a park ranger. Now this ranger fixation set the stage for most of my early life. It determined what books I read, what games I played and what I watched on television or at the movies. Mom and Dad even got into the act. They'd remind me when a ranger-type television show was being broadcast. They'd share newspaper and magazine articles that concerned rangers and national parks. I breathed, ate and slept rangers. As I got older, the "park ranger" dream became more specific. I wanted to be a national park ranger at Yellowstone National Park.

I graduated from high school and found a college in rural central Maine that caters to people who dream of careers that focus on the natural world. These are careers as park rangers, game wardens, outdoor recreation specialists, wildlife biologists and foresters, etc. Tiny Unity College in Unity, Maine was my choice of higher learning.

There was not much to this small college in 1982, though I'm sure it had a little more than it did in 1966 when the first batch of students arrived. Fancy architecture and well-groomed landscapes do not guarantee a quality college. It's the excellent professors and staff who make Unity College special. There was no "park ranger" degree program offered at the time. I didn't want to solely study forestry, wildlife management or outdoor recreation. But, Unity College worked with me and I was able to graduate with a Bachelor of Arts degree in Interdisciplinary Studies with an emphasis on Park Management (that's how they worded it). Basically, I was able to study from all the disciplines of the outdoors that Unity College offered: forestry, wildlife law enforcement, fisheries, and outdoor recreation. Unity College had produced many a fine graduate by the time I received my degree in May of 1986. And, as my "I wanna be a national park ranger in Yellowstone" dream morphed into

"I'm willing to be a park ranger anywhere I can get a job" dream, I stumbled upon Maine's Baxter State Park.

A seasonal campground ranger at Baxter has a working schedule that runs roughly from early May to late October. I was oh-so-fortunate to work at Baxter during the seasons of 1986, 1987, 1988 and part of 1989. During those seasons, I discovered the many people, places and things that make Baxter State Park unique and grand. There were people like Governor Percival Baxter. Governor Baxter purchased all the land (with his own money) that would become Baxter Park, started a trust fund for park operations—and, then, gave all of this to the people of the State of Maine in perpetuity. No matter how many times I read about or visit Baxter State Park, I always think, "Now, there was a man with vision. Thank you, Governor Baxter!" There are others who have become legends in Baxter Park lore like Roy Dudley and Helon Taylor. And there are the good people I was fortunate enough to know personally while I worked at Baxter like Bob Howes, Bernard Crabtree, Greg Hamer, Scott Fisher, Buzz Caverly and many others.

There are special places that are held dear to me like Upper Togue Pond, Sandy Stream Pond, Blueberry Knoll, South Branch Pond, Davis Pond, Northwest Plateau, Nesowadnehunk Stream, South Turner Mountain, Russell Pond, Wassataquoik Lake, Index Rock and a myriad of others. Things such as the great Pamola, moose, bears, eagles and black flies are all vivid memories.

In the following pages, I've tried to convey a little of what it was like for a young man from Connecticut living out his dream. The stories are true as I remember them. They depict what I experienced and what I felt. Hopefully they offer a little insight into what makes a good ranger. All the book learning and degrees won't do it. You need to experience it, too.

There's many a fine book out there dealing with Baxter State Park—Katahdin, the trails, the wildlife and the history. I won't even attempt to bog you down with details you can find from one of those well-researched books. This is just not that kind of book. Historian John W. Neff, in his comprehensive book *Katahdin—An Historic Journey*, writes in his introduction "those who have visited Katahdin have been profoundly affected by the mountain". It's a simple statement that rings so true for many visitors. I still love that mountain and Baxter State Park and return often with my family to camp and hike. However, there's another draw for me. It's the people I met during my Baxter years—people I consider friends. These are the people who still carry the torch for Baxter State Park. This book is dedicated to all Baxter State Park employees—past, present and future.

CHAPTER 2

COURTESY OF NASHVILLE AND THE BOSTON RED SOX

Throughout the winter and early spring of 1986, I struggled to finish my last semester at Unity College in Unity, Maine. In addition, I was trying to gain a paid internship for the coming summer to complete my degree requirements. "Paid" is the key word, as I really couldn't afford to work for free. My first area of choice was the White Mountains of New Hampshire. Truthfully, the White Mountains were the only mountains I really knew. I'd been visiting and hiking in them with my parents ever since I was a young child. I felt comfortable with these mountains. I figured working there during my internship would be an easier transition from college to the real world than working elsewhere.

The White Mountains turned me down. If I remember correctly, the wording in the reply to my inquiry went something like "we don't do that sort of thing here." Whether they meant "we don't do internships—period" or just *paid* internships was never clarified. My college advisor, Wilson Hess, sagely suggested I contact Baxter State Park, particularly District Ranger Bob Howes. Bob was a graduate of Unity College many, many years before my time. With Bob and Wilson's guidance, I was able to work out a plan for my internship.

I was to develop and conduct a weekly campfire talk program for campers throughout the summer in the southern district of the park. The purpose of the program was to provide interpretive, educational and entertaining information essential to the public's understanding of Baxter Park and it's unique status. It would cover Baxter's history, flora and fauna, trails, and mountains and simultaneously educate park users to accept more responsibility for their personal safety while in this wilderness area. I was also challenged to use my program to sway visitor interest from popular

Katahdin to lesser-known areas of the park. At the time, I knew nothing of Baxter Park. However, this was early April. I had until July to get the program ready.

In the interim, I would have to study this great park's history and its flora and fauna. I would also have to personally hike and familiarize myself with many miles of park trails. In return, Baxter Park would house me free of charge in some old camp on the shores of Upper Togue Pond. I would even receive a small stipend to help in the grocery department. It was not exactly a paid internship, but I wouldn't have to worry about rent or the requisite three squares a day. But, lo and behold, Baxter Park had several campground rangers' positions for hire that summer. I had no experience whatsoever in the field of rangering. I hadn't even officially received my degree in park management. But it was still my dream. I applied and was fortunate enough to reach the interview stage.

Here I was, a young college grad-to-be with (what I considered) clean-cut looks and mannerisms. Luckily for me, Wilson Hess took his college advisor role seriously and advised me on proper interview style and etiquette. I visited the local barber in downtown Unity shortly thereafter. It also wasn't long before I helped the stockholders of the Gillette razor company with a timely purchase at the Unity drugstore.

Now, if you look on any map, you'd see that Unity, Maine, is pretty far north compared to most other towns in New England. It's not far below the 45th parallel. And mid-April usually sees the last of the snow except deep in the hemlocks out of the sunlight. Although in the same state as Unity, Baxter State Park seems to be in its own climatic zone altogether. Winter still has a firm grasp on the park most Aprils. Wintry conditions confronted me as I headed north to Millinocket and Baxter headquarters for my ranger interview. It could have been mid-January for all I knew and I was supposed to start my internship in three weeks regardless of my ranger interview outcome.

Of course, many job seekers covet state and federal positions because of the steady work and pay, good health benefits, paid holidays, vacations and sick time usually provided by these positions. This is especially true with the game warden/ranger type jobs. Competition is fierce for all of them. Looking back through the haze of time, I remember very little about my job interview with Baxter State Park. What I do recall was being nervous and a little fidgety when I sat at the end of a long conference table. There were two or three people on each side of the table and one facing me from the other end of the table. Bob Howes was one of the interviewers.

And, though I'm sure they asked me more relevant and important questions, the only question I can actually remember was the one that asked if I would agree to maintain a clean-shaven appearance. Baxter Park, it turned out, had a policy that forbids rangers from having an overabundance of facial hair during the warmer months. "No, not at all," was my curt answer, as I fingered my Tom Selleck/Magnum P.I. 1980's style moustache. You tend to agree with anything the interviewers say when you're trying to land your first ranger job. Then, with the interview completed, I returned to Unity and waited.

It was maybe ten days before Unity College's graduation ceremony when I got a phone call. It was Baxter Park Chief Ranger Chris Drew. Baxter Park was offering me the job as Campground Ranger at Togue Pond. "It was a very tough decision, Steve. It came down to you and one other person. What tipped the scales in your favor was your landscaping experience. Your main duties at Togue will be to put your landscaping skills to work and complete an erosion control project there. Togue Pond is just a day use area. There will be no campers. Do you accept the position, Steve?" Chris asked. You all know my answer or else there'd be no stories of my Baxter ranger days to tell.

"Ok, Steve, the campground ranger season starts on May 10th. Just report to park headquarters on that day to fill out paperwork and the like." Hmm, there was a slight pause on my end.

"Ah, Chris, May 10th is the day of my college graduation. I won't be able to start then," I said apprehensively, thinking they'd give the job to the other guy if I didn't report to Baxter on the date expected. "Well, when would you be able to start, Steve?" Chris asked. We agreed that I'd start Monday, May 12, 1986.

Early Monday morning, with what little I owned piled into my green 1980 Chevy Citation, I made my way back to Baxter headquarters. I filled out the necessary forms and questionnaires to become a State of Maine employee. I even joined the Maine State Employees Association union agreeing to have union dues deducted from my pay. I did this thinking it was a requirement for state employment though I learned later I was spending money for nothing. I was given several Baxter Park Ranger uniform shirts (though not enough for a week's supply of daily changes into clean shirts), a Baxter State Park badge, and a nametag for starters. I was sent to Epstein's in downtown Millinocket to purchase a couple of pairs of green Dickies (courtesy of Baxter Park) to complete my ranger uniform.

With a brief stop at the local IGA, I headed northwest out of Millinocket on what they call the state road. It's really just an offshoot of Route 157. At Togue Pond, I was to meet Baxter Ranger Loren Goode who would assist me in settling in a camp and getting me started on my ranger duties. Togue Pond is only twenty miles away from Millinocket though maybe 300 feet higher in elevation and is really two ponds. Baxter Park owned maybe 12 or 13 camps and buildings on Upper and Lower Togue Ponds. In 1986, the park leased the land from the Great Northern Paper Company.

This land wasn't even within the boundaries of Baxter State Park. At the time, I was a little disappointed. I didn't feel like I was a "real" ranger. I felt more like just another worker hired to perform duties with a pick and a shovel. All those years I spent dreaming and studying to be a ranger just to dig in the ground. Those were my thoughts as I was driving towards Togue Pond. As I turned right onto the Togue Pond road from the state road, I was beginning to think I might have short-changed myself. Was this really what I wanted?

There were still big snowdrifts alongside the road and as I entered the spit of land that separated Upper and Lower Togue Ponds, the drifts became bigger and more numerous. Ice chunks were still floating on Upper Togue. The wind was roaring out of the west across the pond. Waves were crashing loud enough that it seemed I was at the ocean shore. This was May 12th and usually high spring in most places, but not here.

Ranger Goode drove up shortly after I arrived. He seemed like a nice enough person as he pointed out the several old camps along the shore. He said that I could have my pick. He suggested that I spend the rest of the day getting moved in and acclimated to the area. And, if I wanted, I ought to go on up to the gatehouse and say hello to the gatekeeper rangers. "The camp that's right next to the gatehouse is your supervisor's. His name is Bernard Crabtree. Prob'ly be wise to introduce yourself to him later on in the day. You already know Bob Howes. His camp's on the left just before the gate. See ya 'round." And, with that, Loren left.

Early May in Baxter Park is fairly quiet as far as people traffic is concerned. Later on, the Togue Pond area would seem like civilization compared with the rest of Baxter Park. But, on that cold day in May, my first as a Baxter Park ranger, I felt very alone. It was extremely quiet with no traffic. The only sound was the constant wind blowing off Upper Togue. I was just coming from four years of college where I always had people (especially friends) around me. There was always someone to talk to, someone to do something with. There seemed to be nothing like that here.

Well, Ranger Goode said that I could have my pick of camps so I started poking around. Most of the camps seemed very old and were located fairly close to the shoreline. Four of these camps were situated about twenty feet above the pond on a high bank that was extremely eroded. Tree roots protruded everywhere and little gravel and dirt deltas washed into the pond up and down the shoreline. I surmised that this was some of the shoreline my landscaping skills were hired to repair.

Each camp was built with logs and had a screened-in porch. Each consisted of one large room with a little pantry off to the side. At one time, the pantries must have housed a propane stove and refrigerator, but they were empty now. The location of these camps was perfect. The view across Upper Togue took my breath away. There was mighty Katahdin to the north. Big, puffy clouds obscured its higher elevations but I knew what they hid.

"VIEW OF KATAHDIN FROM TOGUE POND"

There were three more camps up the shoreline almost at pond level. These camps were very large and also lacked stoves and refrigerators. Besides that, they lacked views of Katahdin and they seemed rather ratty. But there was one camp set off the shoreline a ways on the high bank. It provided a slightly obstructed view of Katahdin from its screened-in porch, which was filled to the rafters with junk wood. It housed a stove and a refrigerator in a small pantry to the right as you entered the main room. And, off the main room there were two bedrooms. A small woodstove, table and chairs completed the décor of the camp. More importantly, the distance to the outhouse was considerably less from this camp. This was an important consideration when you take into account dark and rainy nights when a long run to the outhouse could cause embarrassment. Oh, that's right. No electricity, no running water (unless I ran it in buckets from the lake), no indoor plumbing—just an outhouse—fifty feet away to the right, just off the porch. This took a little getting used to, considering I just left four years of relatively easy college life with all its modern conveniences and fixings.

As I mentioned earlier, Togue Pond was still owned by the Great Northern Paper Company. Baxter Park owned the camps but leased the land. The intent was to own the land someday and incorporate it into the park as some sort of buffer zone from encroaching civilization. My job as campground ranger was to reclaim and heal the shoreline damaged by years of neglect and abuse. Togue Pond is situated at the southern entrance to Baxter Park where the road forks. This made my position handy to other campgrounds in the park and I could easily fill in when needed. The right fork leads eight miles to a dead end—Roaring Brook campground. The left fork is the 40-mile or so tote road that runs along the perimeter of the park. Along the way, this road passes several campgrounds and leads to Mattagamon Gate at the northern entrance.

Now, my title was Togue Pond Campground Ranger even though there was no longer a campground to range on. My main focus was to regenerate the shoreline, keep the day use area clean and supply the public outhouses with paper and air fresheners. If I'd been assigned a real campground, I would have had an assistant campground ranger and perhaps a few trail crewmembers to work with. As it was, I was in charge of only me. I, in turn, reported to Park Ranger Bernard Crabtree. Bernard had been the long-time campground ranger at Russell Pond. He had just been promoted to a year-round position. And at first glance, one would think that Bernard was a cold, hard man who didn't put up with any nonsense. And, its hard enough making friends with anyone when first starting out. It looked bleak for me—an "outtah state-tah college boy". However, it wasn't long before I discovered what a no-nonsense, *warm*-hearted man Bernard is.

"AUTHOR WITH RANGER BERNARD CRABTREE"

Bernard reported to Bob Howes, then the South District Ranger of Baxter Park. Park alignment has since changed and I have no clue what Bob's title is today. Suffice it to say that ole Bob is up pretty high in the ranks. Now, Bob seemed to always have a soft spot for me. Was it because we're fellow graduates of Unity College? Or was it because I helped pay half of his son Kenyon's first year of college? Remember now, I had no running water. No running water translated into a lack of shower facilities. And, during the summer of 1986 at Baxter Park, it seemed as if the temperatures got higher than the 60's but two or three times. Togue Pond may have even had ice clinking around all summer if I remember correctly. It wasn't exactly comfortable swimming weather. But Bob, being District Ranger and all, had a nice generator and running water at his camp. Bob and his wife, Jeanne, were kind enough to let me use their shower anytime I wanted as long as I deposited fifty cents into little Kenyon's piggy bank—honor system, of course. Since I have this penchant for being clean, Kenyon could have attended Yale or Harvard. But Bob's soft spot for me was more likely just Bob being Bob. He treats all people with respect and always helps them out when he can.

"RANGER BOB HOWES AND WIFE JEAN"

And Bob, even with all his District Ranger power, still had to report to the Chief Ranger—Chris Drew. Chris reported to Park Director Irvin "Buzz" Caverly who I believe reported to the Baxter Park Authority. As I learned over my brief career at Baxter, sometimes the chain of command was not observed—going up or coming down.

During my first few weeks on the job, I had much to learn. I needed to familiarize myself about the park, its rules and regulations, the things I could and couldn't do as a ranger, the goals for Togue Pond, etc. I also had a set of personal goals that I wanted to accomplish—goals that most rangers set for themselves. I wanted to learn all the fundamentals of park operations, use and improve my public relations skills while in a park setting, and practice the skills necessary to become an effective and reliable park ranger. I believe that when everything is said and done, I met these goals, however, my public relations skills seemed to be lacking in one case later on in my first summer. Bernard worked very close with me right from the get-go. I'm not sure, but maybe he thought I was a slacker. For the first month or so, Bernard was always outside my camp at precisely 7:20 am hollering, "Hello in the camp!" My workday normally started at 7:30 am and went to 4:30 pm barring any emergencies or overtime fill-ins. If I didn't respond fast enough, Bernard would add, "Oh, Steve? You still in bed?" Usually I was not able to respond promptly because my mouth was full of cornflakes.

Early that first season at the park, my job was to make all of the Togue Pond camps "blend in with their natural surroundings." Brown and green stain for the wooden camps was easy enough. When I was through with staining the camps, you had to look twice to be sure you actually saw them. However, there was this hideous cement block building (that became known simply as "the block building") right on the side of the main road. It was pretty much the first thing a visitor would see as he drove into Baxter Park. It stuck out like a sore thumb. Today this building serves as a visitor center. Back then, it was just a dark block building filled with junk. Even if you had stained it brown to 'blend in," it still would have looked like a cement block building—only brown. The higher-ups in the park wanted us to apply a special coating over the cement blocks to give the building a different texture before we stained it brown. I guess the idea was to make the building look like one big brown rock.

If I remember correctly, the coating material was called Thoroseal. You had to mix this milky liquid with this powder in just the right proportions in order to get the proper thickness of the mixture. Too thin and it would just dribble off the walls. Too thick and your paintbrush applicator along with your hand and forearm would get stuck in the bucket. Bernard and I were told to wait until we were fully instructed in proper Thoroseal mixology before we attempted to mix it ourselves. I believe the Baxter Park maintenance department was responsible for that particular class. But, like many a government project, red tape caused delays. Training in Thoroseal mixology was not forthcoming anytime soon.

Weeks went by. Bernard was on his days off which were similar to mine except for Tuesday afternoons. Bernard and his wife, Alice, usually headed home to Monson, Maine. On this particular Tuesday afternoon, the park director, Buzz Caverly, was taking a ride through the park. Coming into the park from the south end meant that Togue Pond would be his first stop. Now, Buzz actually knew Governor Baxter. Most likely, Buzz had a pretty good idea of what Governor Baxter meant when he said that he wanted Baxter State Park kept "forever wild and undefiled by man." Well, that block building, situated on picturesque Togue Pond, was defilement by man if ever I saw one—even if Togue Pond *wasn't* part of Baxter Park yet. And Buzz probably had trouble understanding why the block building was not yet "blending in" with the natural background of Togue Pond.

Well, Chief Ranger Chris Drew was not around. South District Ranger Bob Howes was not handy. Park Ranger and supervisor Bernard Crabtree was somewhere on the Great Northern Paper Company's Golden Road heading towards Monson. There were no links left in the chain of command. So, Buzz questioned me directly about why the block building wasn't "blending in". Three links skipped in the chain of command. But, that's how it should be. Go right to the source to get your questions answered.

"Well, Buzz," I replied. "I can't do it until I'm properly trained in how to mix the stuff." Now, I know Buzz wasn't actually angry or even being impolite. But when your 21-and-think-you-know-stuff, you tend to react say, differently, than you do when you're 42-and-think-you-know-stuff. I'm sure I exuded a defiant attitude of some sort. And, if I recall, Buzz was not alone on his ride around the park that day. He had some VIP's with him. On the way into the park, he may have even been talking up this new campground ranger at Togue Pond and how much work this new ranger was getting done. Seeing the "non-blending" block building first thing may have set him off.

But Buzz was cool, calm and collected—just what you'd expect from a park director. It's funny how the words he said that day, in Bob Howe's garage of all places, (that's where he found me) have sort of given me a motto to live by. Buzz said these words quickly, decisively and without fanfare, hopped into his park service vehicle and continued on into the park with the VIP's. "Steve," he said. "Why don't we concentrate on what we *can* do rather than on what we can't." It wasn't said as a question—more like a challenging directive. Done and done.

Buzz was right. I didn't need to be trained or shown how to mix the stuff. Neither did Bernard. We were intelligent enough to read and follow directions. We could figure things out. We understood trial and error. Well, it wasn't long before I was mixing batch after batch of Thoroseal and slathering it on the old block building. Bernard helped out quite regularly. We worked together practically everyday. It was during this time that I realized ole Bernard liked me and that he figured I was okay. Yeah, for two months now, I had been a rather steady and reliable worker and that had impressed Bernard. But, I still have this sneaky suspicion that my good work habits are not what finally proved to him that I was worthy.

Now, in Baxter State Park, radios and noise like that are really not allowed. Rangers do their best to follow and enforce this rule so that all who come to Baxter for a wilderness experience can have their wilderness experience. Way down at Togue Pond, with no campers, but lots of Thoroseal to apply, a little music goes a long way. So, I casually broached the subject with Bernard. He looked pensive a moment and replied, "Yeah, that'd be okay as long as you don't play any of that kinda music that'll scare off the moose." What specific type of music that will scare away moose was unknown to me, but I had an idea what Bernard meant. I just put on my favorite type of music, which turned out to be Bernard's favorite, too. And, to the strains of Ricky Skaggs' *Cajun Moon*, we proceeded to apply the Thoroseal. Other thorosealing days saw us listening to radio broadcasts of afternoon Red sox games. We are both diehard Sox fans. Of course, in 1986, the Sox broke our hearts along with everyone else's that followed the team. The summer of 1986—the Boston Red Sox, country music and Baxter State Park—now that was living!

CHAPTER 3

CLOSE ENCOUNTERS
OF THE BAXTER KIND

The mother moose was standing by her three-week old calf. She gave me a cold hard stare and then laid her ears back. I could actually see the hair rise up on the back of her neck just before she put her head down and charged. I hollered, "Waugh!" as I ducked behind some low bushes. This was surreal. Barely into my second month as a ranger and a big animal (a very big animal) was angry and running straight at me. And, she could kill me or cause some serious damage with one stomp or flail of her front hooves. I was a ranger for Pete's sake. This isn't supposed to happen to me. The low bushes were not going to stop her and neither was my pathetic yelling. How was I going to explain this in my weekly report? Ah, the luck of a rookie ranger and the naiveté of youth. I (in my convoluted way of reasoning) figured that all of Baxter Park's wildlife would know me as a friend and protector just because I wore a ranger uniform. But, mother moose are not particularly impressed by one's outdoor wear. Nor, as I noticed, do they differentiate between park rangers and park visitors.

It had been a very busy Father's Day weekend at Baxter Park. A large volume of traffic had passed in and out of the Togue Pond gate. It was the first weekend of beautiful, sunny weather and visitors came in droves, happy to spend some time outdoors. Father's Day weekend just so happened to be the time that this particular mother moose decided to bring junior out to see the world. A great little book by Bill Silliker, Jr. called *Maine Moose Watcher's Guide*, comes in rather handy if you want to learn more about moose and their life cycle. According to Mr. Silliker, moose are born from late May to early June and weigh close to 30 pounds at birth. If a calf survives its first summer, it can weigh upwards of 400 pounds by late autumn. Although a full-grown moose can look a little gangly and ugly to some, there's no doubt baby moose are cute.

**"COW MOOSE NEAR
DAICY POND"**   **COW MOOSE AT STUMP POND"**

Mama had decided to use the small grassy area behind my camp as her temporary home. The problem was that her temporary home could be seen quite easily from the road. And for visitors, what's a trip to Baxter Park without a moose sighting, right? The Togue Pond road had only recently been paved as far as the area of my camp. At that time, there were no speed bumps on the road in front of Camp Natarswi as there are today. Camp Natarswi is a Girl Scout camp on Lower Togue Pond situated a quarter mile down the road. So, without speed bumps, visitors sometimes drove much faster than they should have as they approached the park.

I'd always hear the traffic coming long before I could see it as the vehicle tires hummed loudly on the asphalt. Then there'd be a louder thump as the drivers realize (a little too late) that the pavement ended. In their rush to the gatehouse, their vehicles would bounce from the pavement onto the gravel in a spray of dust and a hubcap or two. Here, the gravel road runs between Upper and Lower Togue Ponds with Upper Togue on your left as you head towards the gate. Driving along, you can see both ponds simultaneously.

It turned out that I had to run interference for the moose all day. Visitors needed to be kept a safe distance from mama and her baby. When people see a moose, they tend to lose their common sense (note the beginning of this story). Although the visitors were polite about it, they constantly harassed these roadside moose. People coming in and out of the park just had to get a picture of the duo. Mama moose exhibited surprising patience with the crowds considering junior was so young. If people ventured too near, mama just nudged her little one into the woods and out of sight for a while. So, all in all, the visitors were happy and the moose were tolerant.

As the day began to wan and traffic slowed to a trickle, I breathed a sigh of relief and headed to my camp. After a hard day of rangering, a young, single ranger like me had lots to look forward to in the culinary department. Usually a can of spaghettios or Campbell's chunky soup, sopped up with a half loaf of bread and washed down with a quart of milk, would do the trick. After eating, I took a peek out of the back window of my camp towards the grassy area. It was nearing dusk, but still light enough to see mama and baby bedding down. I felt a kinship with them. After all, I was a ranger and Baxter Park was my home, too. Besides, hadn't I protected them from the throngs of people chasing after them all day? Surely mama wouldn't mind if I came out to say goodnight.

I eased near them, feeling good about myself. These moose were friends of mine and obviously they thought themselves safe enough with me to bed down in my back yard. I started talking to them in that voice we humans use when we talk to our pets or our newborn babies. You know that voice I'm talking about. At first, mama and baby just lay there, flicking their ears at mosquitoes and late-day black flies. However, there must have been a trip-wire that I set off, an unseen border, a line I shouldn't have crossed. This is when Mama stood and laid her ears back. This first warning went unheeded. I was her friend, the ranger, so not to worry. Then, the hair rose from the back of her neck. I still didn't get the message. So, Mama charged. I yelled as I dived behind some pucker brush. It's good stuff for scratching your skin, but kind of useless as shelter from a charging moose.

Mama turned to my left just as she reached me. She was so close that I could have punched her in the jaw with a sharp right cross. She circled and returned to her calf's side. With the hair on her neck still standing menacingly, Mama moose looked at me as if to say, "Now, that was just a warning, young man. The next one's gonna hurt!" Given this chance, I backed out of harm's way with a lesson learned. All wildlife needs space and one mustn't encroach on that space or you may find yourself in a dangerous situation. Mama had been patient all day with the crowds, but her patience had been worn down and I was the last straw.

Living and working in a place like Baxter Park doesn't mean you'll always have close encounters with wildlife. Nor will all encounters be as stimulating as the one with mama moose. But, when living in such a wildlife-rich place 24/7, one is bound to meet up with one critter or another. And if not the critter itself, then you may see the signs it left behind. Now, my first two or three weeks at Togue Pond were spent alone. I mean, I worked with other rangers during the day, but at night or on my days off, I was alone as none of the other dozen or so camps were occupied. No electricity and no TV. No telephone either and this was the era before cell phones. I had to occupy my time in different ways. Sometimes I would sit on my porch, listen to the loons wail on the pond and watch the sun go down. Maybe I'd pick a tune or two on my six-string or catch a Red Sox night game on the radio station out of Houlton.

During that first month, the weather was cool, damp, cloudy and miserable. I had to stoke the woodstove every night to keep warm even though it was May. The black flies were just starting to get bothersome. But I was getting used to being alone. I was actually starting to like my solitude when Bernard informed me that a newly hired gatekeeper was going to share Togue Pond with me. I had to *share* Togue Pond with a stranger? Not this boy. I was enjoying the nights after the traffic ceased—*alone*. The loons seemed to be singing only to me. This new guy could set up quarters in one of those ratty camps that had no stove or refrigerator. He wasn't moving in with me. I had to de-mouse, de-louse, de-junk and de-bug my camp by myself when I arrived. He could do the same. In reality however, Baxter Park expected rangers to double or even triple up in camps as staff housing was at a premium.

It was a rather dark and dreary day soon after when I saw this beat up 1970's era, white Dodge Ram pickup. It seemed as if the guy driving was lost or looking for something. He saw me and drove over where I was working. As it was, I was working in front of his future camp. The guy was the new gate ranger. He introduced himself and I did likewise. Dave Tardiff had a big smile and you couldn't help but like the guy right off. So much for wanting to be left alone. I was glad to have a new friend at Togue Pond. Dave shared my camp until he could get his camp into move-in condition. Dave seemed to be a pretty smart guy even though he was married and ten years older than I was. He liked the idea of rangering and looking for "griz"—our term for black bears. Of course, we borrowed that term from Will Geer's character in the classic movie *Jeremiah Johnson*.

"RANGER DAVE TARDIFF"

Speaking of griz, Baxter Park had closed its trash dumps just the previous year. In their place, dumpsters were set up at each drive-in campground and a local trash hauler would empty them on a regular basis. Today, Baxter Park has a carry-in/carry-out policy. But, in the mid 1980's, the park was just starting to move toward lessening man's impact on the environment. This meant no more dumps for starters. No more dumps meant potential bear problems as generations of black bears had gotten used to the free eats the dumps provided. Most bears did the smart thing and foraged for natural foods. Others would sniff around campsites and steal a steak or bag of chips left on a picnic table by an unwary park visitor. This behavior would get these bears into trouble. Both visitors and bears needed an education.

Down at breezy Togue Pond, there were no campers, but there was a trash dumpster. Bears are crafty and actually pretty nimble with their forepaws. One such bear kept prowling around the Togue Pond beach area where the day-use dumpster sat. Every morning as I did my cleanup rounds, I'd see fresh bear tracks all around the dumpster and dusty bear prints on the dumpster lids. It seemed like a small bear based on its print size. I couldn't catch it in the act. This could have been because the bear was dumpster diving in the middle of the night when I chose to sleep. Dave, who was now settled into his camp just a few yards from mine, was also unable to catch the mischievous bear. That is, until one night.

"I kept hearing this knock-knock-knocking," Dave explained. "I couldn't figure out what in the world it was or where it was coming from. The noise would stop and I'd start to doze off again and then knock-knock-knock." Dave seemed to think that the strange noise was coming from somewhere near his porch. Maybe it was a low-hanging tree branch brushing his camp in the night wind. Dave was beginning to think he was dreaming it all. He put on his hiker's headlamp and stepped out into the Togue Pond night to investigate.

Nothing. Barely a breeze, too. "Can't be a tree branch then," Dave thought to himself. "What the heck? I know I heard something." All was quiet on Togue Pond. This strange activity went on for three nights in a row. Each night, Dave was awakened by a mysterious knocking sound that only he heard. His camp was close to mine, but far enough away that I wouldn't have heard anything anyway.

Lack of sleep was getting to Dave. He began to get suspicious that some critter had set up shop in or under his camp. Was it my dumpster bear? No tracks—no sign of bear at all. Finally, when his days off arrived, Dave decided to wait up in the dark and catch whatever it was in the act. Of course, Dave wasn't able to stay awake all night. And, while in a deep slumber, he was once again awakened by the knock-knock-knocking. And, once again, he was unable to pinpoint the source. The next day, however, Dave was up early. There was barely light enough to see by and fog shrouded the Togue Pond area. As Dave was stepping off the porch for his morning run to the outhouse, he heard a scramble under him and saw a black flash. It was a small black bear kicking up pine needles as it scurried away. Dave hollered and clapped his hands, hoping to add a little speed to the bear's flight.

It turned out that my little dumpster bear had been making a day nest under Dave's camp—sort of a bed and breakfast arrangement. A little home-cooked dumpster meal and a cozy little bed on scenic Togue Pond. The ground sloped just right in front of Dave's camp and that made it easy for a person or a bear to crawl under and be out of sight. Once discovered, my dumpster bear/Dave's knocking bear, disappeared. We never saw that bear or any signs of him again, although I thought he had returned one night later that summer.

A few weeks after Dave's sleepless nights, I was awakened by a strange sound. It wasn't a knock-knock-knocking, but rather a whack-whack-whacking. Being the shrewd rookie ranger I was, I surmised that our bear was back and was checking out the accommodations under my camp. While not as roomy underneath as Dave's camp, my camp did offer quality comfort to the discerning bear. But, like Dave, I saw not a thing. So, back to bed I went. Just as I drifted off—whack, whack, whack. Hmm. Maybe it was Dave playing a prank. He sometimes worked the 4pm to midnight shift at the gatehouse and he wasn't above causing me a little grief. A quick glance at Dave's camp through the porch screen showed his parking spot empty. Besides, it was only 11:30 and Dave was still on duty. I went back to bed again, but sat up and waited. In less than ten minutes, I heard the whacking sound again. It sounded like it was coming from the roof area where the pantry and porch walls met to make a ninety-degree corner. My camp was odd-shaped. A main room led back to two bedrooms making a square footprint. But, off of this square, the pantry and porch made a nice corner outside where I kept brooms and rakes out of the weather.

This time, the whacking sound didn't stop. I tiptoed through the main room, opened the front door and stepped out on the porch. The whacking sound was coming from right there! I quickly shined my light up high on the pantry-porch corner. A broom handle, seemingly of its own power and free will, was hitting the outside of the camp—first one wall, then the other. I pushed my head against the screen just enough so that I could see the ground. And there, holding onto the broom with all four paws was a raccoon. He paid me no mind. He was biting and clawing the broom in a way that reminded me of a housecat with a ball of yarn. As he bit and clawed the broom bristles, the handle swung back and forth whacking one corner then the next. "Yah! Get outta there!" I'm still not sure what attracted this raccoon to my broom or why he felt the need to wrestle with it. But my voice must have scared him immensely because he never returned as far as anyone knows.

Now, refuse dumps were history within Baxter Park. But just down the road from Togue Pond, maybe five or six miles by road and two miles as the crow flies, there was a dump. The privately owned campgrounds just outside of the park used it. It was called Abol Dump. And, as the veteran rangers told me, this was the ideal place to go around dusk if you wanted to see lots of bears. True, watching bears roll around in man-made trash does not a wildlife experience make. But I had always found bears fascinating and being able to see them (even in a dump setting) was cause for excitement. So, one evening early in the tourist season, I made my way to Abol Dump. I went incognito, of course. This was not Baxter Park jurisdiction and I didn't want to bring attention to myself wearing a ranger uniform and driving my park-issued truck. I motored to the dump in my green Chevy Citation decorated with Connecticut license plates. I'd look like any other tourist.

As I pulled into the dump, there were several vehicles parked alongside one another. They faced straight ahead toward a big hole in the ground. All that was needed was a giant screen showing the latest release from Hollywood and you'd have felt you were at a drive-in theatre. I eased up near a big four-wheel drive pickup. I felt like a low rider next to such a big truck, but I hopped over to my passenger seat, rolled down the window and greeted the folks in the truck. There were two couples close to my age in the cab. They said they were locals from Millinocket and that they liked to come out every so often and watch the bears. They seemed like nice enough people, but I could smell that they liked to do more than just watch bears when they parked at that dump. I politely declined their offer of a drag on the illegal substance they were smoking. There was no sense mentioning I was a ranger either.

"So, where are the bears," I asked them. "Watch the tree line up on the hill just behind the dump hole. You'll see a couple come down before long," the driver responded. And, almost on cue, a female with two small cubs came waddling out of the trees and down into the hole. The topography of the dump area sloped down from the tree line to the vehicles. The interior of the dump hole, though lower than we were, was hard to see because we were situated on the low end of the hill. Every so often, we'd get a glimpse of the bears pawing around or ripping a trash bag open. All of a sudden, the mother bear and cubs reared up on their hind legs and looked toward the tree line. In a blink of an eye, they were gone. A few seconds later, a very large male bear loomed out of the darkening woods. Ah, mama bear knows best. Male bears have been known to be cannibalistic and fresh little cub makes a tasty treat to a big male. Wildlife biologists suggest that males sometimes prey on cubs so that the females will go into heat and the males can pass their genes on instead. The big bear shuffled down into the dump hole and went to work. There must have been some good eats as the big male really went at it for about twenty minutes.

By this time, my new friends from Millinocket and I were the only folks left watching the bear. The driver got out and tried to attract the bear with some bread. He went right up to the lip of the dump hole and dropped a couple slices. He worked his way back to his truck, dropping a slice here and there as he went much like Hansel and Gretel. I didn't think the bear would come out for plain white bread, but he did. The bear followed the bread trail to the truck. The driver threw a couple more slices, which drew the bear even closer to us. Then he threw a slice out onto the truck's hood. Was he crazy? The big bear only seemed to get bigger as he came closer. Wow! The bear stood up on his hind legs and rested his forepaws on the hood just as a person would do standing at a bar ordering a beer.

"BIG MALE BLACK BEAR READY TO ORDER HIS MEAL ON THE HOOD OF A BIG 4-WHEEL DRIVE"

Remember, this was a huge, four-wheel drive truck and its hood would be right around neck level to you and me. This bear towered over it. The Millinocket folks were really having fun at this point. Slice after slice they threw to the bear. The bear nonchalantly licked up slice after slice. Then, a miscue. One of the girls made a weak throw. The slice of bread landed closer to the windshield side of the hood than the bear's side of the hood. The bear kept reaching and pulling with his paw, but the bread was just out of his reach. One second the bear was standing on its hind legs—the next he was standing on all fours—on the hood! He got his bread. My Millinocket friends kept flicking bread slices out at the bear on the hood. Pretty neat if you ask me. All was going well until my friends ran out of bread. Suddenly, that windshield seemed very thin. The bear slapped at the windshield. He wasn't really aggressive about it, but he wasn't taking "no" for an answer.

Finally, the driver laid on the horn. Poof! No bear. He was gone—off the truck, into the dump hole, out of the dump hole's far side and into the woods. My Millinocket friends laughed and said it happens every time. Then, they started their truck and left. I hopped back into my driver's seat contemplating whether I should go, too. It was dark by now and you couldn't see much at a distance unless you put your headlights on. Besides, it was kind of stuffy with the windows rolled up. You needed the windows closed or the mosquitoes would make bear watching—well, unbearable.

It was kind of spooky just sitting at the bear dump—in the dark—all by myself—even if I was a park ranger. But I thought that I'd wait a little longer. It was so quiet that I could hear the mosquitoes whining outside, trying to get in the car. Then, I saw him. The big black bear that loved bread, but was not too fond of truck horns, was right there looking at me through my driver's side window. Glass, don't fail me now. He just stood there maybe three feet away on all fours. His back was higher than halfway up my window. He was huge. He started walking around my car. I watched him through my driver's side rearview mirror. He sniffed at the rear tire and went out of sight behind my car. I turned to watch him out of the back window. I felt like a diver in a shark cage with a great white shark swimming around me. The bear made his way completely around my car. Satisfied that I had no goodies, he went back into the dump and out of sight in the darkness. It was quite the thrill for me, but I was glad I wasn't in a tent at the time.

I may have seen this bear once more that summer, though it was more likely a close relation of his. I was on the road that led to Abol Dump when I saw this massive black bear crossing the road. His back end was still on the side of the road when his nose reached the center. When I neared the spot where he had crossed at, I stopped, hoping to catch a glimpse of him. He was a bold bear. Most bears would have been long gone and hard to find. This bear was sitting on his haunches next to a big gray boulder right on the side of the road. It was as if he were waiting for me. He looked as if he were a little peeved that I had made him rush his trip across the road. I swear his ears were the size of catchers' mitts. He gave me another look, sort of shrugged, and melted away into the forest.

Dave and I became good friends and enjoyed hiking and canoeing together on our common day off. And many evenings we'd make a run to the bear dump to watch the bears. But as the tourist season heightened, parking space was limited. Sometimes, it seemed that tourist brains were limited, too. Many a time, Dave and I witnessed tourists getting out of their cars trying to feed the bears by hand. Fools. We would tolerate this as long as the adult tourists endangered only themselves. One evening, we finally had to speak up.

This almost seems too frightening to be true, but trust me, it happened. A fellow, his wife, and small child pulled up in their car to look at the bears. They were out-of-staters, no doubt. Which state? I'd rather not tell. Suffice it to say that these people would be considered boneheads no matter which state they came from. They put their little girl (who couldn't have been past the toddler stage I'm sure) out on the lip of the dump with a granola bar in her hand. The parents wanted a picture of her feeding the wild bears! I also remembered vividly the big bear that came out of the pit for white bread. Dave and I felt sure we were going to witness a tragedy.

I had read somewhere that a black bear had been clocked at 37 miles per hour. I don't know about that, but I can say with certainty that a black bear can run faster than 25 miles per hour. Coming home to Togue Pond late one night, I surprised a black bear. I was doing 25 mph as I turned onto the Togue Pond road. For some reason the bear decided to run in front of me on the road for fifty or sixty yards. He was pulling away from me when he finally veered off into the woods! Maybe thirty yards separated this little girl from the two bears in the dump. The parents were the same distance behind her waiting to take the picture. If the bear decided to hurt the girl, who do you think would reach her first? Dave couldn't stand it any longer. He got out of his truck and hollered, "Hey! A guy got his arm torn off last week doing the same thing! Are you crazy?"

Now, either the parents suddenly came out of their never land dream world and realized that bears can be dangerous or they really believed Dave's made-up story about the one-armed guy. Whatever the case, they quickly grabbed up their little girl, piled into their car and left like their very lives depended on it. It's amazing that during the time I was at Baxter, we never heard of one of the dump bears actually hurting anyone. I'm sure there may have been close calls. But you can't blame the bears. They are opportunistic when it comes to food and they can get a tad more aggressive than usual once they connect people with a food source. Within a couple of years, Abol Dump was closed for much the same reason that Baxter closed its dumps.

Another interesting encounter I experienced was just outside of Baxter Park along the west branch of the Penobscot River. I had driven up the paper company road known locally as the Golden Road. This road follows the river for many miles and I used it often to drive up to Ripogenus Dam. Then I'd follow the road back to Togue Pond and watch the whitewater flow or the many fly fishermen cast into the swirling eddies. And as darkness approaches, it is a good area to spot moose. One evening as I was returning to Togue, it started to snow all of a sudden. Bright white flakes floating down in June! But it was 70 degrees. The flakes came down so quickly as I drove that I actually needed my windshield wipers on. It was what they call a "hatch". Thousands, maybe millions of moths had all hatched simultaneously and I had run right into them.

There are all sorts of animals in and around Baxter Park. Coyotes, bears, moose, bobcats, white-tailed deer, red squirrels, pine martins, raccoons and beavers just to name a few. I've mentioned a few "meet and greets" that I've had with mother moose, bears and raccoons. But there is no encounter in the Maine north woods quite like that of a big, 1200 lb bull moose in the height of the rut. Mama moose, for all practical purposes, may be the most dangerous animal to face when she's protecting her young. And black bears, though they can eat you if they want, usually run away long before you even see them.

But the true monarch, the real head honcho, the big boss of the woods is the male specimen of Alces alces—the bull moose. This is especially true from mid-September through the end of October when bull moose do the moose equivalent of searching the honkytonks and bars for a friendly female companion. According to Mr. Silliker, a full-grown bull moose can stand 7 feet tall at the shoulder and measure 10 feet tip to tip. The males grow antlers yearly—starting in the spring. Throughout the spring and summer, the antlers are soft and covered with a substance called velvet. There are many blood vessels coursing through the velvet to feed the antlers-which can grow up to an inch a day. As the rutting season approaches, the antlers turn bone-hard and the velvet sloughs off. The bull moose helps the process by scraping his antlers in the brush. He also does this to show others how tough he is. A bull moose in his prime can have a rack over five feet wide that towers ten feet off the ground. Bull moose tend to have blinders on during rutting season. They are looking for one thing and one thing only. Sometimes they focus only on what's directly in front of them. They put foraging for food behind foraging for a mate and can lose up to 30% of their body weight during the rut. One such bull crossed paths with me in the fall of 1988.

"BIG BULL MOOSE AT WHIDDEN POND"

I had been on my days off and was returning from Chimney Pond to Roaring Brook after a long day hike over Katahdin. Anyone who has climbed up and down Katahdin from a roadside campground knows the last two miles of the thirteen-mile hike can drag on and on. As you near Roaring Brook campground, its namesake brook makes itself known near the trail with loud tumbling and splashing. I was hiking alone, with my head down, just wishing the darn trail would end. I was beat. I put a little extra mileage in on that hike and had pushed hard to beat sundown as darkness comes earlier in the fall. It's a bit over three miles to Blueberry Knoll in the North Basin with a small backtrack to the Hamlin Ridge trail and almost two miles to the top of Hamlin Peak and the Northwest Basin Trail junction. Two more miles via this trail and the Saddle trail gets you to Baxter Peak. The Knife Edge is a mile of rough but fun going over the arête of Katahdin. The Knife Edge has an added feature of a drop of over two thousand feet on either side. From Pamola Peak to Chimney Pond via the Dudley trail is another 1.75 miles and then finally the long drawn-out 3.3 miles of the Chimney Pond trail gets you back to Roaring Brook. When you're young and the Little Debbie snacks haven't caught up with you yet—you can do anything.

I was concentrating on putting one foot in front of the other with Roaring Brook noisy in my left ear, when I heard a loud snort much like one a horse makes. Coming up the trail toward me was a big bull moose with a rack of mythic proportions. It's one thing when you see a moose up to its belly, feeding in a pond and quite another when you see a moose on level ground with you. You are looking up, up and up. It seemed this big bull was tall enough that I could have walked underneath his belly. It was late in the rutting season, but I'm sure he was still on the prowl. Until he snorted, I had been unaware of him and he seemed unaware of me even now, although I was in plain sight only thirty yards away. Had he not snorted, I might not even have looked up. We could have had a surprising and unpleasant meeting. I thought that if I made a little noise, he might give me the trail so that I might get my long hike over with. What was I thinking? Big boss of the north woods give way to a puny human? Hah! He heard me and looked up and I'm sure he saw me, but he never broke his walking-pace stride. He continued toward me nonchalantly. He wasn't charging—he just wasn't going to get off the trail.

I dropped my backpack right where I stood and decided the wise thing to do was to scramble up a spindly hemlock on the trail's edge. There really wasn't anything closer as this was a slightly open section of the trail and I didn't know if by running that I would actually induce the bull to charge. I wasn't taking any chances. The bull continued to shuffle purposefully up the trail until he reached my tree. I was just barely out of antler reach. He actually looked up at me, snorted contemptuously, put his head down and turned off the trail right there. He crossed Roaring Brook, scrambled up the far bank and disappeared into the forest. Wow! That was the closest I'd ever been to a big bull moose. I didn't even need a zoom lens. I hopped down and tried to lure him back into sight with a couple of fake cow moose calls. He didn't fall for it and I didn't get a picture, but I had plenty of adrenaline flowing by then and the rest of the hike flew by.

Cow moose are no angels during the rutting season either. Many times the ladies will let loose with a rather sick-sounding, low frequency, bugle-like call. This is to alert all the eligible bulls within earshot that she is ready for you-know-what. She's in estrus, boys, and it's now or never. Now, if there's only one bull around, he's the lucky one. Even if there are two or three bulls in the neighborhood—if one bull is decidedly the bigger bull—he gets the girl. Sometimes a couple of bulls will do a little posturing by tipping their antlers toward one another or thrash some bushes to show the other guy how tough he is. Usually the smaller of the two will use his wits and bail out before any blows are thrown. But, every now and then, two bulls of equal size and strength will converge on the same cow or claim the same pond. In Baxter Park, a bull moose has to prove his worth to the lady or she won't be going home with him.

Before Bernard became my supervisor in Baxter's front country, he had been the campground ranger at Russell Pond deep inside the park. On one of our Little Debbie snack breaks, I noticed a large set of antlers at Bernard's camp. It was labeled "The Loser—October 1979". Bernard told me the story behind "The Loser" between bites of Little Debbie oatmeal cookies. With apologies to him, I'll try to tell the story the best I remember it. It can be considered a twice-told tale and if it's anything like twice-baked lasagna, it might be better than the original. If you'd rather read Bernard's original tale, please see Mr. Silliker's book. My version is how I remember Bernard telling me the story.

Bernard and his wife, Alice, loved working and living at Russell Pond as the true essence of Baxter State Park can be found here. From Russell Pond, it's about a seven-mile hike south to Roaring Brook campground; a nine-mile hike north to South Branch Pond campground and another nine mile hike west to Nesowadnehunk campground. Going due east out of Russell Pond gets you no where but lost as that direction leads only to the park's eastern border and from there to the East Branch of the Penobscot River. If you cross the river, you might make it to Maine state routes 11 or 159 and the town of Patten. It's a lot of rugged country sprinkled with camps and outdated logging roads. Read Donn Fendler's book *Lost on a Mountain in Maine* and you might get an idea of the remoteness of the Russell Pond area even for Baxter standards.

The only man-made vehicles that get into Russell Pond today are floatplanes in the summer and snow sleds in the winter. Cars and trucks can only go as far as the trailheads. Russell is a quiet and reflective place. I, for one, can honestly say that you haven't been to Baxter Park until you've visited Russell Pond and its environs. One has to work hard in order to get to Russell. And you are going to get wet. There are no more footbridges across Wassataquoik Stream when you come in from the south. Sometimes the stream is friendly and only knee deep. Other times, it can be treacherous and over your head. The ranger at Russell will even close the trail when the Wassataquoik is on the rampage. But when you finally get to Russell, you are about as far as you can get from civilization in the eastern U.S. With a love of solitude and nature, Bernard always said it was difficult to accept his promotion to a year-round ranger's position because he had to give up his gig at Russell.

Anyway, on the October day in 1979, Bernard became aware of a noisy scuffle in the campground. It was very loud, but scuffle doesn't quite describe it. It was more like a thunderous, no-holds barred brawl. Two big bull moose were going at it, trying to gain the affections of the local cow. It seems these two bulls had been giving the evil eye to each other for a couple of days and things finally came to a head. More likely than not, if two bulls clash antlers over a female, it'll be a brief spat. The smaller or weaker of the two knows he's not up to the task and bails out before any real harm is done except for bruised pride. The winner gets the girl. The loser heads to the next pond hoping to meet another cow in estrus. He also hopes that she'll be alone. Sometimes, just showing off antlers to one another is enough to decide things. Size does matter in the moose world.

"COW MOOSE IN THE SHADOWS OF KATAHDIN"

The two bulls that Bernard heard thrashing and crashing were very equally matched—height, weight, age, and antler size. Neither was going to run after antler swaying at twenty paces. And, neither was going to give ground at first antler clash. These bulls were young, aggressive brutes, and nature was driving them hard to get the girl. Bernard said that after the fight, the ground looked like a bulldozer had been through—saplings two inches thick were snapped and the ground was torn up like a freshly tilled farmer's field. It was quite awe-inspiring, Bernard always said, but a little scary, too. Here were two, beautiful, big animals really hammering away at one another—snorting and blowing and bellowing to beat the band. This was truly a ferocious fight. Neither bull gave ground. Or if he did, he'd gain it back and then some.

As I remember it, Bernard said that he lost sight of the battle in the thick undergrowth around Russell Pond, but he could still hear the struggle for a while. Then, all was silent. He heard one bull snort. Bernard dared not go into the scrub to investigate—not yet anyway. Those bulls were ramped up and in the fighting mood. Anything or anyone could induce a charge. An angry bull moose, full of rut frustration, is no animal to trifle with. But, Bernard was still a young ranger in his early forties and his curiosity got the better of him. His curiosity really grabbed hold of him when he saw one of the bulls stagger into view a little way down the pond shoreline to claim his mate. Bernard just had to know what happened. So, with a little trepidation, Bernard started following the fight path into the scrub. Wow! What a fight it must have been after the bulls went out of sight. Bernard could not believe the destruction those two animals wrought with their north woods war. As Bernard continued to follow the signs of the fight, he noticed the terrain started to slope gently downward. He was breaking out into a cold sweat, figuring any minute to be charged by the loser hiding in the brush.

As Bernard neared a small drop-off, he saw quite a sight—the other bull—dead. "Now, how could that have happened?" he asked himself. Even with two bulls of equal strength, the odds of one killing the other were very high. Bernard surveyed the ground and tried to piece together what happened once the bulls took their fight out of view. It seems that one bull was unlucky enough to have swung his backside downhill as the two bulls reached the sloping area right before the small drop-off. Bernard believed that "The Loser" lost his balance while his antlers were still entwined with the winner. As "The Loser" lost his footing over the edge, the weight of his own body snapped his neck—much as the noose does to a human's neck at the gallows once the trapdoor is sprung. It was kind of bad luck all around for the loser.

It was not a pretty sight, but it's nature at its most raw. A step in another direction or if the fight had gone elsewhere, then maybe the loser wins or at least loses without getting killed. Baxter State Park is that wild of a place for both man and beast. Don't take your safety for granted here—it's not guaranteed. And, don't push your luck. You'll run out of luck long before nature gives in.

CHAPTER 4

RODEO BULLDOGGING— BAXTER STYLE AND THE BEAR DOGS OF KATAHDIN

Baxter State Park is a wilderness area of over 204,000 acres in which hunting is not allowed except in small, specified areas that Governor Baxter agreed to in order to purchase the land. But Baxter State Park is surrounded by privately owned paper company lands full of moose, black bear, deer, and other assorted Maine wildlife. And hunting is allowed on these lands. There is a marked park boundary, but many Maine mammals tend to have a deficiency in reading and comprehension and have trouble recognizing the park boundary. Northern Maine is a big-game hunter's paradise. Folks come from all around to hunt moose, bear, deer, etc., etc. during legal hunting seasons. And black bear hunting in northern Maine draws 'em right in. Now, as rangers, we felt kind of protective of the flora and fauna within the boundaries of Baxter State Park. We even had a little sympathy for those critters that chose to live outside Baxter. Of course, there wasn't much we could do about their choice of living arrangements.

My old ranger buddy, Greg Hamer, was once the campground ranger at Roaring Brook Campground. As I've told you previously, I was the campground ranger at the newly acquired Togue Pond. At this time, camping wasn't allowed at Togue Pond. I was, more or less, the "landscape architect," hired to replant, stabilize, and regenerate roughly twelve hundred feet of Upper Togue Pond shoreline. This shoreline had been sort of ignored, abused and tortured over the past century until there was really no shoreline left—just truck tire tracks left from folks driving their pickups right into the lake so they could wash and rinse their vehicle all in one convenient spot. At least Greg had campers he could practice his rangering skills on. I first met Greg on just my second day as a Baxter ranger. He was about my age but was already into his second season as a ranger and no longer a rookie. He liked to think he knew more than I did about Baxter Park and its environs. He did. But I did my best to show him otherwise.

Well, one fine September day in 1986, ole Greg came bouncing down the eight miles of dirt road that separated Roaring Brook from Togue Pond. He'd come to enlist my help with some new scheme he was always coming up with. Now, my first inclination (whenever Greg asked me for help) was to reply sarcastically, "Help? Help with what?" You'd have answered much the same had you worked with Greg for any length of time. Several instances would come to mind whenever he would come bouncing into my dooryard in his ranger truck.

There was the time he claimed he needed help with some light janitorial work at Rum Brook picnic area and at Avalanche Field group camping area. "Light janitorial work" turned out to be shoveling out the pit outhouses. In front country areas, the public outhouses are usually sucked clean by the septic man and his giant hose. However, that only works in the new-fangled cement-vault outhouses. There were several outhouses that were just a seat, four walls, and a roof situated over a hand-dug pit that collected all the campers' and picnickers' leftovers. As these pits filled, they needed to be emptied every few seasons by hand. They were very small buildings and not really attached to anything. So the idea was for one of us to slightly tip the outhouse while the other shoveled out the fun. Of course, Greg thought he could shame me into doing all the dirty work. He tried to make me feel like it was my duty to shovel all four of the outhouses especially since I was a first-year ranger. Well, my mama didn't raise no fool in Connecticut, boys. I suggested I'd shovel the first two and Greg would do the last two. Agreed.

Well, it turned out that my two outhouses really didn't get much use and most of the "fun" had composted nicely into a peat moss-like matter that really didn't smell bad at all. Greg was hunched over, supporting the slightly tipped outhouse on his back, laughing the whole time. He obviously thought I had it rough. Then it was on to the final two outhouses—the heavily used outhouses at Avalanche Field—and Greg's turn. Lots of campers and transients used these outhouses. They were constantly in use. New leftovers were added almost 24/7. Yep, Greg's turn. With a little help from a come-along winch and nearby tree, we tipped the first one over so Greg could get at the "honey". Let's just say it was very fresh, very fragrant and very soupy. It was not Greg's finest hour. It was even a little rough on me when a well-placed gust of wind would share with me all the freshly stirred up outhouse fragrances.

Another example of Greg's sneakiness was the time he came roaring into my dooryard at Togue Pond (at midnight, mind you), claiming he had caught a nuisance beaver or some other mellow mammal in an aluminum trash can. I don't recall the exact animal he claimed he had. He had the trashcan (full-sized and complete with lid punctured with breathing holes) on the seat in his truck cab. Greg said he needed my help to release the animal. Not yet knowing how Greg operated, and thinking that this was real ranger work, I eagerly offered my assistance. We climbed into the truck cab, the aluminum trashcan between us, and Greg said, "Take the lid off and take a peek inside, Steve." There wasn't much sound coming from inside the can so I slowly canted the lid to one side to peek in. All I saw, in the dim glow of the cab light, was a mask-faced critter with a pointy nose whose mouth was opened, exposing sharp little teeth, coming right out at my face. I let out a loud, "Waugh!" and proceeded to slam the lid back down. To this day, I have this feeling that I probably pinched that raccoon's front paws between the lid and the can much like you would your fingers in a car door. Greg fell out of his truck with laughter. As you can imagine, I wasn't all that amused. Neither was that raccoon. After Greg picked himself up off the ground, brushed the pine needles out of his thick red hair, and settled down enough to drive, we released the nuisance coon where he'd find it difficult to pester campers or anyone else for that matter.

Now, getting back to that particular September day in 1986—in answer to my query about what he needed help with, Greg replied straight forwardly, "We need to catch some bear dogs running loose between here and Roaring Brook." Since I was an "outtah statuh" with limited bear dog-hunting experience, and the fact that we were in Baxter State Park where domestic critters are not allowed, I prodded Greg to explain how these bear dogs got here.

"Well," he said, "folks come up from away and they hunt black bear with hounds. They have radio collars on the dogs to keep track of 'em. Around here, the hunters—who usually own the dogs—hire a Maine guide. They'll start chasin' a bear somewhere between Patten or Staceyville and the East Branch. 'Course the bears can be pretty smart. They head west towards Baxter Park and give the dogs the slip once they reach Katahdin." I guess the local black bears had more schooling in reading and comprehension than some of the other big game animals—seeing how they were smart enough to run into the park and out of the hunting zones. As it turns out, the dogs give the hunters and guide the slip in much the same way—once they get lost in Baxter.

"I try to catch them every fall and help the hunters out," Greg continued. "The dogs are tired and the owners are worried. And besides that, the dogs don't belong in Baxter." So, we hopped into Greg's ranger truck, and proceeded back toward Roaring Brook Campground along the dirt road where the bear dogs were last seen.

Well, it wasn't too long before we spotted the first one stumbling along the edge of the road. As soon as it became aware of us, it started casting its nose about looking for bear scent—or so it seemed. I had a feeling this dog thought we were its owner. Was he trying to impress us with his keen sense of smell and devotion to bear-hunting duty? I'm not sure. But it reminded me of how most human workers act when the boss shows up unexpectedly. We stopped. I hopped out and called to the dog. It came right to me, a little worn down and haggard, but unhurt when all was said and done. I lifted him up into the truck cab between Greg and me. There's nothing like the smell of an outdoorsy-type dog that's been on a bear trail for several days—especially in a small and enclosed area.

Greg stabbed the truck into gear and away we went in search of other wayward bear dogs. Our first dog was extremely chummy for a bear dog. I really didn't know what to expect as far as bear dog behavior towards strangers went. Then again, he was the first bear dog I'd ever met. He got excited as the three of us spotted one of his compadres in the middle of the road moving at a trot. We applied the same technique for capturing this one as we did with the first. But this bear dog never stopped, slowed down, or even looked back. He just sort of kept going at the same trot.

Well, we knew these dogs were tired and worn. Some of them really will attempt to continue tracking until exhaustion drops them. Greg and I didn't want to lose this one in the woods. That's when Greg came up with the idea of bear dog wrestling. He said that he'd seen something similar on television once where a cowboy would ride his horse chasing a steer. Then he'd jump off the horse, land on the steer's back, and wrestle it to the ground. "Here, you drive and I'll get on the hood," Greg suggested. "Just as you catch up with the dog, hit the brakes. I'll slide off and land on the dog." It seemed like a good plan at the time.

I hopped into the driver's seat and Greg deftly positioned himself horizontally across the hood of the truck. I put the truck in gear, eased off the clutch, and tromped on the gas pedal with my new bear dog pal riding shotgun and baying encouragement as we slowly caught up with bear dog number two. We're only talking maybe six or seven miles an hour. I never had the truck out of the granny gear.

And, as Greg planned, just as the front of the truck obscured my view of the running dog, I hit the brakes. Greg slid off the hood and, for all I knew, landed under the front wheels. A little dust, a cuss word or two from Greg, and bear dog number two was on his way down the road at even a faster clip. Greg stood up and brushed himself off. "Fire her up, Steve! Let's try it again!" And away we went.

You'd think that bear dog number two would have run off into the woods. But, looking back, I think he was having fun being the chasee instead of the chaser. Eventually, Greg's steer-wrestling trick worked. With two loudly baying hounds in the cab with us, we rolled into Roaring Brook campground. We radioed park headquarters and had them contact such-and-such a guide to come out and pick up the dogs. The dogs had ID tags with the owner's name, address and number along with a temporary ID tag with the local Maine guide's information.

About an hour and a half later, a truck pulled up with Virginia plates. It was the owner of the dogs coming to claim his dogs. The truck was like a kennel on wheels. To this day, I'm not sure how he got past the gatehouse and into the park with five other hounds in his truck. Must have been professional courtesy of some sort. With the remainder of the pack baying loudly throughout the campground, the owner thanked us for corralling the other two dogs.

Being an inquisitive ranger, I asked him about hunting bears with dogs. It turns out that bears don't like being chased. The Virginia hunter went on to say that sometimes the bears tree right away. Sometimes a bear will lead the dogs astray and give them the slip in Katahdin country. Why, there are even a few bears that will stop and fight and give a dog a good swat or two. The hunter showed me one dog that was healing up from such a swat. His whole side was raked to the bone, but being a bear dog, he still acted kind of spry. After a few more handshakes and another check on the dogs, the hunter and dogs left.

Now, as a one-time event, this bear dog rescue wouldn't even register. But I know that Greg wrestled many a bear dog on September days in the coming years—at least until he transferred to a back country campground. It became a tradition of sorts, and as far as I know, no rodeo cowboy ever wrestled a steer faster than Greg wrestled bear dogs.

"AUTHOR WITH BEAR-DOG WRESTLING
RANGER GREG HAMER"

CHAPTER 5

THE MOUNTAIN HAS SECRETS

Katahdin, with its steep, rugged trails and fickle weather, determines whether you can climb its heights on a given day. Or worse, Katahdin decides whether you'll return safely—or not at all. At 5267 feet, it is a mere bump when put alongside massive North American mountains such as Shasta, Rainier, or Denali. What it lacks in height, Katahdin makes up for in its steepness, remoteness and climate. Its closest trailheads are over an hour's drive from the nearest hospital and town of Millinocket, Maine. Millinocket is a solid six-hour drive north from southern New England's population centers of Boston, Worcester, Hartford and Providence. Heading north or west from Katahdin just brings you deeper into the Great North Woods of Maine. And eastward lies the small towns of Patten, Stacyville and Grindstone. Katahdin is truly a long way from anywhere.

"KATAHDIN"

The climate on Katahdin's heights is similar to that found on the tundra 1500 miles north in Labrador. At the 3000-foot level, trees give way to krummholz, growth-stunted trees ranging in height from ground level to 3 or 4 feet. The height of the krummholz does not indicate the tree's age, as much of this type of vegetation can be over a hundred years old. As you climb higher, the mountain landscape is just Katahdin granite covered with lichens and rare artic plants. If you didn't know any better, you might think you were really standing on the Labradorean or Alaskan tundra. This area of Katahdin is known as the Tablelands. Caribou roamed this area up until a century ago and several attempts at reintroducing them have failed.

Snow can fall every month of the year on Katahdin. My very first climb to Baxter Peak and subsequent crossing of the Knife Edge found me bundled up against a snow squall on June 18th! There are sheltered areas on Katahdin where the snow never melts and if you find these places on a hot and humid summer day, you feel blessed. The mountain has secrets and it can be fun to explore its nether lands. Park policy forbids off-trail hiking for good reason. One way or another, you will be injured, lost or even killed. Even when you stay on the trail, these things still happen. Going off the trail only multiplies the chances it will. It's as simple as that. Getting lost is no picnic. Again, see Donn Fendler's book *Lost on a Mountain in Maine*. You'll get the idea.

Some rangers like to go off trail or bushwhack. Keep this to yourself. No need to let the brass know. The rangers who bushwhack are trained for this sort of thing and they always leave an itinerary with another ranger. I've never attempted a major bushwhack alone on Katahdin's slopes. Never. As a matter of fact, I've only completed three major bushwhacks and they were all with an old ranger buddy of mine named Scott Fisher. Scott has since been up 14,410' Mt. Rainier in Washington State and 22,834' Aconcagua, the highest peak in South America. Bushwhacking Katahdin is exciting and adventurous and you never know what you'll see or find. Most often you find that you will never attempt to bushwhack that particular area again. Along with the fun and adventure come scratches, bruises, scrapes and maybe a broken bone or two—if you're lucky. You can be prepared with a Katahdin topographic map and compass and still end up lost or come out miles from where you thought you were. Bushwhacking is not for the uninitiated and should never be done on a whim.

"RANGER SCOTT FISHER"

I completed one such "on a whim" bushwhacks with Scott one late spring. It was attempted after we'd already hiked nearly seven miles from Roaring Brook campground to Chimney Pond campground, up the Cathedral trail, and over the Knife Edge to Pamola Peak. As we started our decent to Roaring Brook via the Helon Taylor trail, we decided (on a whim) to take a hard left and bushwhack off Keep Ridge to Pamola Pond a few thousand feet below. We were carrying our Baxter Park topographical maps, flashlights, and ranger bravado. The plan was to stop at the remote Pamola Pond and then cut through the forest to the Chimney Pond trail and follow that back to Roaring Brook. As soon as we stepped off the Helon Taylor trail to start the bushwhack, my left boot sole ripped apart from the boot uppers exposing my toes to the rough topography. With the sole flapping every step, Scott and I clawed through the krummholz. Scott led the way, as I was a little slower with my "flat tire". Sometimes I'd lose sight of him if one of us fell into a hole hidden by the krummholz. We ended up in a rocky stream (which was actually Pamola Brook) that we thought would lead us to Pamola Pond. The stream led us to where it crossed the Chimney Pond trail about a mile above Roaring Brook.

Greg was the campground ranger at Roaring Brook at the time. He thought he might have needed to organize a search party for us. We were lucky—that's it. Scott and I made a very serious error in judgment that day. The most serious was going off the trails and not letting another ranger know our plans beforehand. Had we really gotten lost or hurt while bushwhacking on a whim, rangers would have had no clue where we were. We had signed in on the hiking registers at the campgrounds. But then we deviated from our plans so radically that it would have been as hard to find us as it is for finding the proverbial needle in the haystack.

I've done other less risky bushwhacks on Katahdin with my wife, Pat. These were minor treks and probably wouldn't even count as "real" bushwhacks and we shared our plans with Greg before we set out. They were off-trail nonetheless and that adds an element of danger and risk. Katahdin bushwhacks should never be attempted without proper preparation, and unless you have wilderness skills, patience, and stamina, I would advise against ever going off-trail. I wouldn't want to be accused of promoting a delinquent hiker lifestyle. Bushwhacking is inherently dangerous to you and to anyone else who may have to rescue your hide if you screw up.

Katahdin is steeped in folklore from the local Abenaki Indians all the way down to the current local residents. It's very name, Katahdin—the very way the name rolls off your tongue—demands respect (again, you should see John W. Neff's *KATAHDIN, An Historic Journey* if you want more detail on this aspect of Katahdin). There's even a legend amongst some rangers that ghosts of humans past inhabit the camps and roam the trails around Katahdin. Anyone who is familiar with Baxter Park is well aware of the great Pamola who lives on the heights (read Jane Thomas' *Chimney Pond Tales* to learn more about Pamola's origin and subsequent conversations with famed Baxter ranger Roy Dudley).

Pamola, as legend has it, can take a beautiful, calm and sunny day and turn it into a dark and stormy night with a snap of his fingers. And if he takes a dislike to you, you may find it hard to get off the mountain unscathed. I brought my father, Joe, on a Katahdin expedition early one summer while I was a Baxter ranger. Now, my father was not the typical hiker. He smoked, he drank, and he worked hard. That was the extent of his physical training.

But he wanted to see for himself if Katahdin could live up to the billing I gave it. So, I decided to take him on the most difficult route I knew of at the time. And at that time, I was not aware of Pamola and how anti-social he could be.

"AUTHOR'S DAD, JOE, DEFYING
PAMOLA ON KATAHDIN"

Katahdin's trails are tough, steep and mean no matter which way you choose to climb. But the trails out of Roaring Brook and Chimney Pond tend to be the toughest with the Cathedral, Dudley and Knife Edge trails leading the way. And, that's the way I led my father. Now, what my father lacked in hiking ability he made up with determination and a "won't quit" attitude. It helped that he didn't bring along his cigarettes that day. He made it fine along the first 3.3 miles to Chimney Pond. The next 2.5 miles straight up the Cathedral trail was another matter. He kept asking me why we didn't follow a Boy Scout group going up the easier Saddle trail. I told him if he was going to hike Katahdin, he might as well go whole hog. The Cathedral trail has a way of weeding out those who smoke too much. It didn't help that my father's one-quart plastic canteen sprung a leak and he lost all his water when we were no longer near a handy water source.

I constantly encouraged my father to keep going, that we were almost to the top, not much further, Dad, blah, blah, blah. I thought it was my leadership and coaching that helped to prod him along. Years later, he claimed that there was a beautiful woman hiker in red short-shorts just above us on the steep slope. He maintains that it was this woman who led him to the top. I never saw her. No matter who you are, no matter how old you are, no matter which trail you followed to get there—reaching the top of Katahdin is a proud accomplishment. It's the getting down that truly beats the hell out of a hiker. This is where Pamola comes in.

Once a hiker commits to crossing the Knife Edge, he is exposed to wind, lightning, rain, snow, hail and gravity. There's no place to hide, no place to seek shelter. And it's a long, steep 2500' drop to either side of you as you straddle the trail. Hikers are advised not to start across if the weather is poor or even just threatening. Things looked good as my father and I stepped off Baxter Peak to cross the 1.1 miles of the Knife Edge to Pamola Peak. I think Pamola waited until we were halfway across when he whipped up some clouds and wind. There's nothing like watching ominous clouds scud over the land *below* you, climb ever faster up the steep slope until they clear the mountain and go over you, and then descend the far side of the mountain and lock you in a white fog. I literally hauled my father over the Knife Edge to outrun the impending bad weather. It wouldn't look good for a ranger to let his dad get lost or hurt on the mountain. What normally is an hour's hike took but thirty minutes. Of course, the weather cleared considerably as soon as we started our descent from Pamola Peak onto the Dudley trail. Coincidence? Or was it Pamola's good temper returning once all the people left his heights that day? I considered the score with Pamola even. We'd been allowed to climb and return safely.

Maybe Pamola is more irritable at certain times of the year. Based upon the events of August 1986, I'd have to say that August is not a Pamola-sponsored month. Perhaps it is because August is the time when Baxter Peak is visited most. Pamola has been known to prefer his solitude to crowds. In late August of 1986, I brought a couple of my non-hiking friends along on a day hike. Our plan was to scale Katahdin much the same way my father and I did. That plan was discarded fairly early in the day once my friends got a taste of the trail. Bubba St. Jean and Kevin White were not in Katahdin shape—physically or mentally. Just getting to Chimney Pond was an accomplishment and it would have been unwise to try for the top.

We decided to go up the Dudley trail a short way and veer off on a side trail to Pamola's Caves. Though not caves in the true sense of the word, Pamola's Caves are fun to prong around in. They are really just giant granite slabs that lay this way and that. At certain points, you do feel as if you're in a cave or underground, but you're just under great boulders. The trail leads through this maze of granite slabs and we took our time. Pamola must have felt violated, however. As I was coming down a slanted granite slab from a small ledge, my foot caught and caused me to fall a short height of just two or three feet. I fell awkwardly and believe it or not, broke both my right thumb and right foot where the big toe meets the ball of the foot. Needless to say, it was a long and painful hike back to the car. Dipping my broken bones in ice cold Chimney Pond helped somewhat. Pamola won that day, but at least he let us return home. He hadn't been as benevolent just two weeks earlier.

"Unit 12 to Chimney Pond," came the call over the radio. Static. "Unit 12 to Chimney Pond," the voice repeated, this time with more urgency. "Chimney Pond. Go ahead, Unit 12," answered Esther Hendrickson, the Chimney Pond campground ranger. All park personnel have access to a park transmitting radio for communication. Campground rangers usually have radios in their office and their truck. I had only the radio in my truck, which I kept on whenever I was on duty. The radio is the only way rangers can contact one another or with headquarters. But, unless you heard your campground or your ranger number called, radio traffic was mostly background noise. Most radio traffic was between headquarters and gatehouse or campgrounds and dealt mainly with camping reservations. Sometimes it was ranger to ranger—usually one ranger asking for assistance with a task. Other times, radio traffic reported emergencies. Unit 12 was the number given to the walkie-talkie used by the trail crew member whose turn it was for mountain patrol. Most often, high on the slopes of Katahdin, the mountain patrol ranger assisted disoriented hikers or made sure folks didn't go off trail and trample fragile alpine vegetation. But, one mountain patrol volunteer couldn't be everywhere.

"Esther, I think someone just fell off your Knife Edge." Instantly, every ranger within earshot of a park radio was zoned in on the conversation. Every ranger, whether near the rescue site or 30 miles away on the opposite end of the park, would be quick to respond to a search and rescue if needed. Depending upon the severity of the hiker's injuries and where in the park the accident occurred, most rescue efforts would be controlled by the nearest campground ranger. If the rescue were beyond a seasonal ranger's abilities, he or she would radio the ranking ranger on duty. Usually, in the park's southern end, this ranger was Bob Howes. And, by the sound of Unit Twelve's voice and his description of the accident, Esther was going to need help.

It was a Sunday afternoon in mid-August. It had also been a Class I hiking day—perfect conditions with no threat of bad weather. It was one of only a few days like that in the summer of 1986. There were plenty of hikers on Katahdin and other mountains throughout the park. Some were hiking alone, some in pairs and some in groups. Unit 12 had been alerted that the individual who had fallen off the Knife Edge was part of a large group traveling over the arête. As I've alluded to previously, the Knife Edge is a premier hiking trail curving over a mile from Baxter Peak to Pamola Peak and is close to 2500' above Chimney Pond campground. There are many places along the Knife Edge that are only three feet wide and the drop from either side is dizzying. The trail is dangerous in high winds and poor weather conditions.

On a good day, if you stay on the trail, you really can't just "fall off" the Knife Edge. What the 16-year old hiker had decided was to leave the Knife Edge trail about midway across and attempt to descend straight down to Chimney Pond via the precipitous cliffs. The descent to Chimney Pond from this point looks possible to the untrained eye. At first, the drops are easy to handle and you think you can continue down—until you reach a drop that can only be navigated with ropes and rock climbing gear. You decide to turn around and go back up but find you can't climb up what you just came down. You're trapped.

Katahdin is old, eons old. Not all of its granite is solid. Many of its cliffs are pockmarked with big slabs of "rotten rock". The young hiker was on one of these slabs and the drop down from there to the next level was impossible to negotiate. He was trapped there, as he couldn't get back up either. He hollered up to some of his party above him on the Knife Edge. He said that he couldn't go down or up, that he was stuck. Could they get some help? They had barely turned around to go for help when they heard him scream as the "rotten rock" gave way. His hiking party later reported that they heard him scream twice as he fell. They didn't know how far he fell or how badly he was hurt—or, if he had even survived. They raced back to Baxter Peak where Unit 12 was alerted.

By the time Esther got the call at Chimney Pond, it was late afternoon. There are no marked trails that go directly from Chimney Pond to the area where teenage hiker fell. From the ranger's camp, you have to circumvent Chimney Pond to get to an open field. This alone takes thirty minutes to get around. From the field, you can follow gullies up through the scrub, krummholz and scree. As the glacial cirque that Chimney Pond sits in starts to curve upward, it gets steeper and steeper. In early July, a snow arch usually forms here and is quite spectacular up close. Many trained rock climbers use this approach to get to the various technical rock climbs. These are approved routes on the almost perpendicular cliff faces of the South Basin.

The true, straight up and down cliffs start just above the snow arch location. It's at least an hour's climb in good conditions just to this point. A volunteer completed this bushwhack and reached a point where he could see through binoculars the result of the hiker's fall. The 16-year old had fallen approximately 1000 feet. There was no doubt that this rescue was going to be a search and *recovery*—nobody was alive to be rescued. Things happen fast when events of this nature occur. Park personnel are mobilized and various state agencies are coordinated. Bob Howes contacted the 112th National Guard and put their helicopter crew on alert. He also called volunteer search and rescue teams from throughout the state of Maine that are trained specifically for these types of recoveries.

Bernard and I prepared to hike into Chimney Pond at first light to aid in the recovery. Lester Kenway readied his trail crew to assist in the probable litter carry. But, there would be no recovery that night. Bob made the decision not to put anyone else at risk for a body recovery. If there'd been any hope that the hiker was alive, a rescue would have been started promptly. Esther would have gathered as many volunteers as possible from her end. Other rangers would have driven a minimum of a half hour to Roaring Brook campground and then hiked the 3.3 miles to Chimney Pond. But, he was not alive. The recovery of his body would start at first light.

Bob, Bernard, and I reached Chimney early the next morning. Other rescue personnel were also arriving. The plan was to get hiker's body down to Roaring Brook by nightfall. The long litter carry was the reason Bob had arranged all the help. But, the weather was not cooperating. Chimney Pond was in the clouds and the wind was biting. It was mid-August but there was an early winter feel high on Katahdin. The clouds would break and you'd see the mountain bathed in sunlight. Then, quickly, the mountain was shrouded again. Was Pamola up to his tricks again?

As I followed Bob up the gullies beyond Chimney Pond, he said, "So, you wanna be a ranger?" I knew he said that because I was now experiencing the flipside of moose watching or helping a park visitor find their campsite. This was the tough side—the dangerous side of rangering. As the next 36 hours ticked by, I would see just how unpleasant a ranger's duties could be. The clouds were so thick that I'd lose sight of Bob who was right in front of me. We all had walkie-talkies. I used mine when I lost my way in the fog and with Bob's guiding voice on the other end, I found my way back to the group. Lester, along with the professional search and rescue team, had been trying all morning to reach the body. But, conditions were worsening. The hiker's body was still up high where ropes and pitons were needed to get up and down the mountainside.

Bob was worried that he'd end up hauling one of us out of there hurt if we continued. The cold clouds and wind were wearing many of us down. Hypothermia was a real threat. Bob was in constant contact with headquarters and Chief Ranger Chris Drew. Chris told Bob that since Bob was the ground coordinator and on-scene, it was his decision to call off the recovery temporarily. Chris informed Bob that the weather was to worsen as the day wore on, but clear out overnight. Tuesday looked much better. And, on Tuesday, the 112th Medivac helicopter would be available. It could land on the field on the far side of Chimney Pond, meet the recovery team with the body, and fly the remains to Millinocket. The danger level was too high to risk an attempt to retrieve the hiker's body that afternoon.

Bob called off the recovery, but not before the search and rescue team had reached the body and wrapped it in a padded, orange-colored bag. At this point, all rescue personnel were called off the mountain until daybreak. Most stayed at Chimney Pond in the ranger's camp or in the bunkhouse. I decided to return to Togue Pond, sleep in my own bed, rest up and then return first thing in the morning. As it turned out, I didn't have to hike back after all. Bob set it up so that I flew into Chimney Pond with the 112th crew. The day was bright and sunny and I'll never forget the sight of Katahdin from the air as the helicopter cleared Keep Ridge on the northeast side. Coming into Chimney Pond, the South Basin's walls seemed to close in. I felt sure the rotors would clip the cliff walls, but it was just an illusion of closeness. Where we landed on the far side of Chimney Pond is almost a half-mile from the steep walls.

By the time I arrived with the helicopter crew, the recovery team had managed to get the teenager's body down the steep pitches to a point where a litter team could carry him to the waiting helicopter. The descent from here is still steep but didn't require ropes except for one traverse along a large boulder face. I don't remember why or how I was chosen or if I volunteered, but I was to be the park representative accompanying the body in the helicopter back to the Millinocket airport. The boy's parents were waiting there.

I remember that I was a little scared. The dead hiker was all wrapped up but I knew that he'd been alive just forty-eight hours before. I didn't even want to imagine what the 1000-foot fall did to his body. Lester Kenway helped wrap him in the padded bag. He saw what happened and described it once. We never asked him again. But the most vivid memory I have of this whole sad story was landing at the airport. As the helicopter approached, I could see two vehicles parked and four people standing nearby, looking ever so small from up high. One vehicle was a hearse, one a sedan. Two people looked to be from a local funeral home. There was no doubt who the other two people were. Even from high in the sky, I knew they were the boy's parents. I could see their sadness and disbelief. As the helicopter lowered, I could see their shoulders were slumped in grief. We landed and the funeral directors came forward and took charge of the body. The boy's parents had turned away by then—I never had a chance to say a word to them. I don't think I could have said anything to comfort them. "Sorry for your loss" doesn't quite cut it in a situation like that.

It was early afternoon on a Tuesday. My two days off would start soon. I got a lift to headquarters to grab a shower and pick up my truck. I was thinking that I didn't like this part of my job at all. The kid was just five years younger than I was. Yes, his death was his own fault, but I couldn't help thinking how many times I had already crossed the Knife Edge and never really felt threatened. The boy was just enjoying a hike on a mountain that hundreds of people enjoyed every day in the summer. He had just misjudged Katahdin and his own ability. I couldn't wait to spend my days off away from the park. I needed to get away.

I was almost out of the headquarters doors when one of the reservation clerks stopped me. She explained that a family was staying at a camp on Clark's Island on the far end of Lower Togue Pond. Remember—no phones, no way to communicate. She needed me to canoe out to the island. There was bad news to deliver. A close family member of the Clark Island family had died. There was no other way to reach them. Someone had to canoe across the lake and report the news in person. Togue Pond was my campground and I was the closest available ranger. Yes, Togue Pond was my campground and even though that part of Lower Togue Pond was *not* part of Baxter Park, I knew it was the right thing to do. It was a family of three on the island, two parents and their little girl. I delivered the sad news as quickly and easily as I could. The father, though shocked by the news, kindly offered to tow me back with his small engine boat. The late afternoon west wind had kicked in. It would have been a long, hard paddle back against the wind. I gladly accepted the tow and wished him well as he turned back after dropping me off.

I stowed the canoe in the canoe shed near the shore. I climbed the steep bank and crossed the Togue Pond road. A couple hundred feet further and I was looking out over Upper Togue Pond. The sun was low in the western sky and the whitecaps on the lake looked more gray than white. Katahdin was there to my right, looming over the pond. The mountain hadn't changed. It still looked the same. Somehow, I had thought it would look different after all this.

"COW MOOSE AT SANDY STREAM POND

CHAPTER 6

OF PRIDE AND PRESERVATION

As the first summer of my ranger career rolled on, I learned many things about Baxter Park, and about myself. What I learned came in handy every Saturday night at Katahdin Stream campground. Bob Howes had suggested that I start my fireside program on the first Saturday after July 4th. He reasoned that with peak camping season arriving, I would likely get a good crowd to attend. I asked fellow campground and gatehouse rangers to post notices that I'd drawn up advertising my program. Katahdin Stream campground was chosen for its semi-central location on the western side of the park. It also had a large, open field common to the rest of the campground. It was close enough to the campers so it would be easy to get to, yet far enough away so that we would not disturb those who'd rather not hear another ranger program.

My first year presenting the program was part of my college internship and was unpaid. By the end of that first season, Baxter Park thought I'd done a good enough job that I was asked to present the program again in 1987 as part of my paid ranger's duties. However, that first year's program was memorable because I was learning as I went. Each Saturday night I tried to improve on the previous week's program. I'd arrive around 6:30 p.m. in my ranger truck and get a campfire going for the 7 p.m. program start. The first few weeks were probably a tad boring for the campers who attended. I basically spouted out facts, figures and history of Baxter Park and not much else. This was stuff they could have read themselves in park handouts. It wasn't all that entertaining, especially when the no-see-ums were biting.

I did spark up a little excitement once during one of the earlier presentations. Talking in front of a group of people about a place that I was just learning about myself made me a little nervous. I kept flicking my Bic lighter ever so slightly while I spoke. The problem was that the lighter was in my pocket and a flick with a little extra on it burnt a hole in my trousers.

The crowd thought it was funny and it did loosen things up a little. The fire safety segment of that talk came across rather strongly. Future talks saw my lighter put back on my truck dash once the campfire was started. And, poor Bob Howes. As my Baxter Park internship sponsor—he had to attend every one of my presentations. I don't recall getting rained out that first summer, or if I was, I may have used Sundays as the rain date. So, either way, Bob was doomed.

But, all was not lost. At the end of each presentation, I handed out surveys for the folks to fill out and critique the program. Basically, I was asking them to give me feedback on what would make the program better. What did they like most? Least? What did they want to hear more of? Less of? And, if they'd be so kind as to drop the completed survey off with a ranger or at the gatehouse as they left the park, I would greatly appreciate it. With input from ranger friends like Dave Tardiff, Bob, Bernard, Greg, Julie and Brian Johnston, Eric Merry and Homer King, I crafted a pretty neat ranger program before August rolled around. I even added special effects and stunts.

Most of my first attendees (bless 'em—they were the guinea pigs) suggested that I include more personal stories about the park and fewer facts and figures. Based on the returned surveys, most of the park visitors believed that the program was educational and worthwhile. Most folks were brief in their comments while others were verbose. A common thread through the surveys was that the campers liked the light banter between Bob and me. Actual comments ranged from a simple "how about marshmallows?" to "this is our third year here at Baxter and the program has enlightened us to the history, politics, wildlife, and surrounding areas. The program was covered well in all dimensions and it would be nice to see this program presented at all the other campgrounds throughout the park". As it was, my program was the first of its kind in the field for Baxter Park—a fact not lost on me. I felt the pressure to do well so I could satisfactorily complete my internship and actually *receive* my diploma from Unity College. And from the park's point of view, the program needed to succeed in educating the public. I'm not sure I'd have the nerve to attempt the creation and presentation of a similar program today at the age of forty-two.

Dave discreetly suggested that I don't make fun of any one state as I might offend some visitors. This was after the very first program when I used a fictional Massachusetts camper to illustrate how not to get lost hiking in Baxter Park. It wasn't long before I enlisted Bob and Dave as special guests. At that time, Bob was the resident bear ranger. He'd been thoroughly trained to safely capture problem bears in and around Baxter Park. He would then release them many miles away in hopes that the bears would behave themselves.

Bob was kind enough to tow his culvert-bear-trap-on-wheels to Katahdin Stream every program. When I came to the bear safety segment, I would turn the program over to him. Bob knew his bears all right, and he enthralled the audience with a few bear tales of his own. I'd have to say that if I had been filling out that survey, I would have noted that Bob Howes' portion was my favorite. Bob would explain the difference between problem bears and well-behaved bears; how he trapped them in the culvert trap; and, what he did with the bears once he caught them. He'd also educate the audience on how they could help all park wildlife by not feeding the animals and by keeping their campsite clean so as not to attract wild critters.

Some of the "special effects and stunt work" involved Dave Tardiff as a special guest. Bob was able to park the bear trap right at the program site and would demonstrate how it worked for the audience. The trap had a steel door in the back that slid up and down like a guillotine. To set the trap, Bob would pull the cable connected to the door to lift it open and connect it to some sort of bait in the closed front end of the trap. The bait would attract delinquent bears that would climb in and tug at the bait. This would release the door, which slammed shut with the bear inside. Dave played the bear on many occasions for me. After the first time, he chose to wear ear plugs as there was really no place for the loud crashing sound to go once the door slammed shut. Dave said his ears rang all night. Sometimes Bob and I let Dave out of the trap promptly. Other times, we were sidetracked by questions from the audience and Dave would have to remind us to set him free.

When a real bear was caught in the trap, Bob would be summoned to the scene. There were several inch and a half holes on the trap walls. Bob could peer into one of these and estimate the bear's weight for the proper dose of tranquilizer. The tranquilizer needle was put on what was called a "jab stick"—a pole that could be slid through one of the holes. And, with a well-placed jab of the stick, (usually in the haunch area of the bear) Bob would get his bears to relax and go to sleep temporarily. Bob would then drag the bear out of the trap; weigh and measure it; determine its sex; and pull a non-essential tooth that was sent to the Maine Department of Inland Fisheries and Wildlife for aging. It seems that you can tell a bear's age by counting the growth rings in a cross section of a bear's tooth much as you can tell a tree's age by counting the rings on a cut log. An ID tag was then placed on the bear's ear.

Once all the scientific stuff was completed, Bob would bring his problem bear to an area where it couldn't cause trouble. In 1985, Bob captured and released 19 problem bears, but during my 3-plus seasons at Baxter Park—none. It was a little disappointing because I love bears and wanted to be part of the bear action, but I was happy that our bear/camper education program was successful. Once relocated, most bears stayed in their new neighborhood. Others returned to the scene of the crime and got into trouble again. These bears had to be recaptured and re-released even further away. One bear did this five times. Bob needed patience with wayward bears, but not as often as he needed it with people—park visitors and rangers alike.

Bob is one of several rangers who have been trained in law enforcement. Bob pretty much has the same power as a state policeman and could carry a sidearm if he chose to. Bob can arrest people who break the law or write them a court summons and fine depending on the crime committed. Most crimes occurring at Baxter were park related; illegal camping, sneaking domestic pets in; harassing wildlife. Sometimes people would break the 20 mph speed limit beyond a tolerable level. Depending on how intolerably the speed limit was abused, the speeder would just get a talking to, get a ticket and fine, or even evicted from the park—regardless if they had a week's camping reservation already paid. Other folks would overdo their drink or drug of choice and become disorderly. But most people were well behaved and enjoyed their Baxter visit. Seasonal rangers like Dave, Greg or me did not have the arresting power that Bob had. However, we could hold someone until Bob or another law enforcement ranger arrived. Sometimes Bob would just wait at the Togue Pond gate for the alleged crime committer and deal with him as he tried to exit the park.

Now, being in the tourist business, Baxter Park does its best to educate people rather than charge them with a crime. Of course, this would depend on which law was violated and how badly it was broken. But, no matter what the crime, Bob had a way with people. He could somehow diffuse any situation even if an individual was out of control. Once, a park patron missed seeing the large and obvious park signs that describe some of Baxter Park's rules and regulations. One sign is 35 miles away on the northbound side of Interstate 95 before the Medway-Millinocket exit. Another sign is at the edge of town just as you leave Millinocket twenty miles from the Togue Pond gate. Plenty of warning. These signs spell out a few of the main regulations like no pets, no motorcycles and vehicle size restrictions.

This particular patron is not the only one to break park laws, but I use him here to demonstrate Bob's skill with people. The patron had brought along his dog in the back of his pickup. The truck had a cap with tinted windows on the side. The gate ranger (it might have been Dave—I don't remember) noticed the dog through the back window of the cap. He tried to stop the guy but he kept driving. Well, Bob was radioed. "Togue Pond to 53?" Rangers have call numbers. I was 72—also known as "the spare number" in the park logbook though I never knew why. Every other ranger had his/her name listed next to his/her call number. My number just read "72—spare number."

"Yeah, go ahead, Togue," Bob responded. The gate ranger briefly described the situation and Bob was on his way. A campground ranger was driving toward the gatehouse from the opposite way and heard the radio traffic. He was kind enough to stop the man and escort him back to the gatehouse. The ranger explained that domesticated animals were not allowed in the park as Baxter Park preserves and protects first and recreation comes second. Well, this fellow wasn't taking "no" for an answer and proceeded to holler at and berate the gate ranger. He was going to camp in the park with his dog anyway. He'd paid his money. It was a public park—blah, blah, blah. He was pretty upset.

Now, in order for you to grasp how good Bob is at this sort of thing, you have to understand that this park visitor was positively irate. To say that he was out of control is an understatement. Bob pulled up in his truck shortly thereafter. In a cheery voice, Bob said, "Well, what seems to be the problem here?" Well, that guy just lit into Bob about the park policy against pets. The gatehouse area can be a little crowded and busy sometimes, what with people entering and exiting and milling around. So, Bob casually walked the guy back down to his park truck for a little private chat.

We couldn't actually hear what Bob was saying to the man, but we saw Bob take out his citation book and write the man a ticket. The funny thing is, the guy was shaking Bob's hand and it looked as if he was thanking Bob for helping him see the light! Did we miss something? Did Bob slip the guy a C-note or something? Nope. Bob is just a natural at getting people who are misguided to see the error of their ways. Bob does this in a manner that doesn't require him to show anger or raise his voice. People become putty in his hands. It's so easy for Bob. Many rangers have told me they've witnessed similar situations that Bob diffused. The alleged lawbreaker always ended up shaking Bob's hand and thanking him as Bob handed him a ticket and fine. Go figure. I could have used Bob's people skills in late September that year. Because I lacked those skills, or didn't have them to the degree that Bob has, I came close to losing my fledgling ranger job.

Unlike today, the Great Northern paper Company owned the Togue Pond area in 1986. With its lease, the park had also acquired a permit from the Land Use Regulatory Commission (L.U.R.C). L.U.R.C. was a state agency that was pretty strict when it came to environmental laws especially with land near waterways. And, it didn't matter if the permit holder was a public entity like Baxter Park or a private individual trying to develop his land in some way or another.

All that summer, I worked hard at reclaiming the battered shoreline of Upper Togue. Seventy-five or more years of abuse and neglect took its toll. Bernard and I worked side by side every day. Many times, Bob would work with us. At various times, we had volunteers for a week or two at a stretch. Boy Scouts from Millinocket worked for a week in June as part of their Eagle Scout program. "Volunteers for Peace" was an organization that brought together young adults from all over the world. They volunteered their labor on projects like Togue Pond around the globe. "Volunteers for Peace" sent a group for two weeks each in 1986 and 1987. The groups consisted of people from the U.S., Italy, Germany, England, and Czechoslovakia just to name a few countries I remember. The Boy Scouts and "Volunteers for Peace" worked diligently and took much pride in what they were trying to accomplish. Most of the European volunteers could speak and understand English much better than I could understand their various languages so communication was not a problem.

It was just a little culture shock for me on the few hot days we experienced those summers, as the European women had no problem jumping into Togue Pond to cool off at lunchtime—sans clothes. And, unlike most American women, the European volunteers saw no need to be clean-shaven on their legs and armpits. Who says rangering in an out the way wilderness area isn't culturally stimulating? But, when all was said and done, I learned as much from them about their countries and cultures as they did about mine. Many of the European male volunteers thought that all American men would be like a John Wayne movie character and act tough and mean. Working with Bernard and me, they saw that most Americans were really a lot like them and we learned most young Europeans had the same outlook on life as we did.

It could be back breaking but rewarding work. Truckloads of tree length cedar logs had been brought in earlier that spring. These logs had to be peeled of bark and sorted by size. The steep and eroded shores of Upper Togue Pond had to be stabilized with vegetation—grass and transplanted trees. To do this, the cedar logs were cut to whatever length was needed and placed along the contours of the shoreline to make terraces. The logs were held in place by cedar posts that were set in the ground by hand at least 2-3 feet deep. These terraces were then filled with bark mulch and soil and seeded with grass. The freshly sprinkled grass seed was covered with hay. The trouble with the hay was that we had 100 bales brought in at the start of the project that was left uncovered to help it decay. By the time the second summer arrived, the hay had become infested with snakes and more snakes! I'd grab a handful of hay to shake and spread over the newly planted grass and I'd end up shaking out seven or eight snakes, too. They were just garter snakes, but spreading hay quickly became one of my least favorite chores.

———

"SOME OF THE CEDAR LOG TERRACE WORK
AT TOGUE POND"

The soil had to be trucked in from an hour's drive away at Nesowadnehunk Field. Bernard and I drove dump trucks 17 miles one way via the Baxter tote road to Nesowadnehunk. Bernard would skim loam from the field with a pay loader and fill the trucks and we'd make the return trip to Togue. We'd be lucky to get three or four trips completed in a day. This was time consuming work, but great care had to be taken in order to meet L.U.R.C. standards. Also, our goal was to make the terraces look as natural as possible with the idea the vegetation would overgrow the cedar logs. Hopefully, in a generation, one would never know it had even been replanted. Over the summer, as slow progress was made, it was becoming a labor of love. I really thought I could see Governor Baxter's vision of preservation first and recreation second. Togue Pond might be part of Baxter State Park someday and I felt great pride that I was helping to heal its shoreline. And, I'm sure I felt a little over-protective of the Togue Pond area as the season wore on.

This particular late September day, I was brushing a coat of brown stain on the "Thorosealed" block building. I was cleaning up my tools when I heard a vehicle wheeling into the rangers' home area. Most park visitors respected our privacy. The people in this truck did not. I looked up and saw a ratty pickup truck being driven much too fast through the trees and tearing up exposed tree roots. The driver then parked the truck much as vehicles had been parked in the past—almost to the water's edge with no concern for the delicate vegetation. This was the grass and small trees we'd just planted that summer to regenerate this part of Togue's shoreline. Three men got out of the truck and started to nose around in front of Dave's camp. Dave was on duty at the gatehouse. Well, I was a Baxter Park ranger and I took my job seriously. I figured I'd best see what these gents were up to and maybe educate them a little about treading lightly in this area. Looking back, I see that I could have done some light treading myself that day.

When you're 22, brash and idealistic, you don't always come across as polite. You get right to the point and throw diplomacy out the window. And I felt a little like mama moose protecting her baby from a perceived threat—my baby being Togue Pond. I was walking briskly towards the group and in mid-stride hollered, "Hey! What're you guys think you're doin'? You don't belong over there! That's private ranger housing!"

As soon as they heard me, they started walking towards me. I had no clue about the sort of mess I was getting into. Baxter Park management had always been protective of the park borders and of the land areas adjacent to the park. Over the years, this protective policy had led to tiffs and legal affairs with paper companies and other land-owning individuals. I was on my way into the latest row. It seems a developer had proposed some plans to build a fancy, upscale outdoor recreation complex pretty much on the park border. The park fought him every step of the way through legal channels. The park was doing its best to keep development from encroaching on its borders. The developer was trying to carve out a niche in the "wilderness experience" business. It's understandable from both points of view, though the developer's "wilderness experience" was one that was complete with all the comforts of home—resort style. Not exactly the type of place that fit in with Baxter State Park's philosophy of preservation first and recreation second. Needless to say, this developer was not too keen on Baxter Park—or anyone who represented the park.

I'd never met the developer in person, but as I neared his truck, I recognized the name painted on the truck door. Since we were close enough now, I didn't holler, but my voice had an edge to it. "Excuse me, but what are you doin'? And, why did you drive in speedin' like that—tearin' up the ground? We're tryin' to reclaim this area and repair past damage." I guess I could have said "hello" and introduced myself first, but I wore a nametag on the pocket of my Baxter ranger uniform—good enough. I'm sure my approach helped to rile these men. One of the two gents with the developer stepped forward and said, "Listen, sonny. Do you know who we are? You can't talk to us like that and we can pretty much drive where the hell we please!" No doubt this was the incorrect approach to take with me. They didn't wear nametags, so of course, I didn't know their identity. His words just added fuel to the fire already burning inside of me.

"I don't care who you are, mister. You don't belong in this area and you have no right drivin' in here as recklessly as you did! I suggest you leave—pronto!" I was none too happy at this point. The developer smiled slyly. He'd decided it was time to introduce his guests. It seems that his "guests" were two Maine State senators. He had recruited them so he could show them what he was up against with the park. Mr. Developer had been squeezed by L.U.R.C. about his shoreline development and he felt the park was getting an easy ride from L.U.R.C. concerning Togue Pond's reclamation. Had he followed L.U.R.C.'s policies? Had he gotten in trouble with LU.R.C? Had he been cutting corners and to hell with the environmental consequences and been called to task? I can't say for sure, but he didn't like it his L.U.R.C troubles and was trying to persuade the senators that somehow Baxter Park was not fulfilling L.U.R.C.'s regulations and should be penalized.

The developer and the senators shall remain nameless though I remember them well. Let's just say that I don't need any legal hassles twenty years after the fact. But, in my *opinion*, those two senators were not representing their constituents or the State of Maine very well. It was politics as usual and money talks. I was just a naïve, young ranger with an idealistic view on things, and maybe I had a slight temper-control issue. No, there was no "maybe" about it if I were to be honest about it. "Bob Howes-style" professionalism was not my strongest asset. Blunt, straight-to-the-point and not exactly diplomatic was my modus operandi. Looking back, a little diplomacy might have saved me much heartache and trouble.

"It doesn't matter who you are. For one thing, your drivin' habits aren't helpin' our reclamation efforts here and if you guys are truly senators who serve the people of Maine, you'd act the part and help protect this park from money-hungry developers like this clown!" I jabbed my thumb at the sneering developer who seemed to be enjoying the bristling exchange of words between the senators and me. Well, my last stab at diplomacy got a rise out of senator number one. "I'll not be talked to like that from any state employee! I'll have your job, sonny! You can count on that!" He jotted my name down in a small notebook he retrieved from his shirt pocket. "You might get my job, but I'm getting you out of Togue Pond!" With that parting shot, I tromped back to my truck and radioed Bob for assistance.

Now, when you talk on park airwaves, every park employee with a radio or any civilian with a scanner can hear what's going on. Sometimes it's a guilty pleasure eavesdropping on the action. So, in order to keep things at a low profile, I answered, "Well, there's a situation here at my camp that needs your assistance, Bob," to his inquiry as to why his presence was needed. Bob got the hint and he arrived promptly. I was still riled when Bob drove up. I explained the situation to him before he strode over to talk to my new friends.

Those senators were very good at slinging the BS. Before I knew what was happening, they claimed that I had threatened them with bodily harm. This outright lie sent me to the next level and Bob asked me to go back to my truck and wait. One minute I was staining a building, listening to a Red Sox broadcast and feeling proud that I was a ranger—and, the next, I'm being accused of threatening government officials. I knew that I'd done nothing wrong. Those senators and their developer buddy were peeved that I'd dare raise my voice to them. The senators also seemed even more upset that I didn't back down when they announced how important they were. Things were not looking good for my rangering career. Bob was able to get the developer and his senator chums to calm down, took notes on their "stories," and sent them on their way. Bob wanted a written report on my take of the episode—pronto. This was a Sunday and by Tuesday, things were only getting worse.

Those two senators wanted my job all right. They went straight to the Speaker of the House in the Maine Senate and then to the governor with their complaints. The governor didn't take things as seriously as those senators would have liked, but the House Speaker did. He was on Buzz Caverly's tail clamoring for my termination. Things looked bleak indeed. Bernard gave me the bad news. I had to drive to Millinocket and see Buzz at park headquarters. How had I gotten myself into this fix?

Here I was in the Park Director's office with my career on the line. I was 22, brash, bold and stubborn and firmly believed that I had only performed my ranger duties as expected. It was just my style that needed a little work. Buzz had drafted a nice, concise letter of apology for me to sign and send to each senator. If I signed the letter, I could keep my job, as the senators were willing to drop their termination suit against me. I read the letter. It was written very well and it would seem the signer of the letter was very contrite for doing his job. If I did what the senators demanded, they would be gracious enough to let me keep my dream job. All I had to do was grovel a little; you know, kiss their asses. Of course, I knew an apology was in order for my general approach to the situation. However, I couldn't shake the feeling that these senators were using their positions of power to bully me. And, I certainly would not apologize for doing what was right for Baxter Park. No, I wasn't signing it.

Buzz looked none too happy as I said, "I'm not signin' it, Buzz," when I handed the letter back. I thought for sure he was going to dismiss me from the park staff right then and there. Instead, he tried to reason with me. I don't remember exactly how he tried to reason with me, but I remember that my answer was still going to be "no." His phone rang before I could continue my refusal to sign. I'm not sure whom he was speaking with on the phone, but I could tell that Buzz was talking to someone who was very angry. Buzz was taking heat from someone. Was it one of those senators, that shifty developer, or maybe the governor? Whoever the caller was, he was raking Buzz over the coals about something. Buzz didn't flinch. It may have had nothing to do with my situation. Listening and watching Buzz handle the irate caller; I realized that the apology letter wasn't about me. It was about Baxter Park.

I was just one of many rangers who come and go over the years, but Baxter State Park was here forever. All rangers are there to preserve and protect the park. We are also there to ensure that the park's integrity and good reputation remained intact. By signing that letter, I'd have to swallow my pride and let those bandwagon politicians push me around. And yet, signing that letter also meant that I would be representing the park in a positive way. Watching Buzz getting hammered on the phone, I knew what I had to do. Of course, I really loved my job. I wasn't being that altruistic to be honest.

Buzz hung up the phone and put his hands together. He didn't mention the phone call he just concluded or the crap and abuse he had just taken from whoever called. He simply said, "So, Steve, what are we going to do?"

"Buzz, I realize this whole thing isn't about me. I love the park and respect the people I work with. I know I was just doing my job, and maybe I should have gone about it differently. If signing that letter will help ease tensions, I'll sign." And, with that, Buzz handed me the letter. I read it once more, signed it and shook Buzz's hand. He thanked me and at the time I didn't understand why.

Well, all in all, I came out of that scrape unscathed. Of course, Bob and Bernard still had their jobs to do. Part of their jobs is guiding wayward rangers. Luckily, when your supervisors are rangers, too, they tend to go a little easier on you. Bob and Bernard wanted me to see the error of my ways, learn from my mistakes and, hopefully, become a better ranger. There was no yelling or hollering. As a matter of fact, I received the "counseling" part of the *Commendation/Counseling Record of Employee Performance Form* that is put in a ranger's incident file, not his personnel file. What difference it makes as to which file it goes in, I don't know. Check with Bob or Bernard.

The Employee Performance Form describes the "task(s), which an employee has done well or poorly". Check one. Bob checked "poorly" and wrote that I needed to be "more professional and polished when dealing with the public in all circumstances. Be courteous, polite and assist whenever possible and don't hesitate to call appropriate supervisory personnel when conditions prevail." Ah, yes. Had I radioed Bob sooner, I probably would have avoided all the trouble. However, I would have missed out on learning things about myself. This incident only confirmed my belief that many politicians are shifty and can't be trusted.

Bob and Bernard went over this form with me a couple days after I had been in Buzz's office. I still didn't agree that I should even be going through all this, but Bob discreetly told me that the only reason I was still gainfully employed was because of the timing of the incident. This happened in late September versus early May. By this time, I had exhibited good ranger skills throughout the season and Bernard reasoned that I wouldn't be making a habit of yelling at people even if they deserved it. I had earned a decent reputation with Bob and Bernard up until the senator affair. Both Bernard and Bob stood up for me and I was lucky that the disciplinary action was as tame as it was.

That's all that saved me from losing my ranger job. I signed the "counseling" form, using the hood of Bob's ranger truck as a desk. Both Bob and Bernard agreed that I had done the right thing as far as my duties went protecting the park. It was just my technique wasn't acceptable and I would need to improve it—drastically. Through rangers like Bob, Bernard and Buzz, I started to see that I represented something unique and far-reaching as a Baxter Park ranger. It was something more important than my stubborn pride.

In the end, that developer was able to complete his outdoor resort on Baxter Park's doorstep. In my opinion, this resort has been a good park neighbor over the intervening years. However, my opinion of the developer's tactics of using politicians for personal gain remains unchanged. I think the tactics were immoral and underhanded. I'd have to check the voting records, but I believe either one or both of the senators lost in the next election and I remember I felt pretty good about that at the time. Or, it may have been just wishful thinking that they were voted out of office. Either way, I still felt good *thinking* that it happened. I was still a ranger, though a blot now stained my record. I had learned a valuable lesson at the steep price of almost losing my job, but I hadn't traded my morals or integrity for it.

CHAPTER 7

BETTER YOU THAN ME

Not everything was doom and gloom at Baxter Park. Not every park visitor behaved as badly as my senator friends. Not every moose, bear or raccoon chased me through the forest. Nor did every black fly, mosquito and no-see-um dip into my blood supply—though it seemed so at times. Many days just passed by and saw only lots of shoreline reclamation at Togue Pond. Bernard and I took a lot of pride in what we were accomplishing and it was starting to show.

Park visitors were enjoying the fruits of our labor as we had constructed picnic sites and a beach area where none had existed before. The picnic sites were nestled under big red and white pine trees that grew along the shoreline. We constructed them with sand walkways and steps that led down to the water. This way all exposed tree roots were covered and most people would follow the nice "path" we made to the water's edge instead of stomping on the newly planted vegetation. We also placed cedar posts and rails in a rustic fence setting to keep traffic from encroaching on the delicate shoreline. Before there had been any control or real care of the Togue Pond area, some people literally drove their vehicles into the shallow water and washed them right in the pond!

Visitors often complimented us on the work we were doing and they were excited that Baxter Park was now looking after such a beautiful area as Togue Pond. Most of the credit should be given to Bernard. He knew how to take the general plans of the environmental blueprints and put them into practical use on the shoreline. It might have been an environmentalist, naturalist or some government official who drew up the plans, but it was Bernard's ingenuity and vision that brought it all together on the shores of Togue Pond.

Bernard could see a nice, sandy picnic spot in the shade of the pines with new grass and trees growing; whereas, all I could see was an eroded landscape that exposed tree roots and bony rocks and made it tough for a visitor to lay their beach towel on. Bernard took his time. He was methodical.

And, he made sure I understood what needed to be done. He wanted me to visualize it, too. I'm sure it pleased him when he saw the light go on in my eyes once I was able to grasp the whole project and how we were going to accomplish it.

Our working relationship actually seemed more like a friendship even though he was my supervisor. We laughed, joked and made fun of each other just like schoolboys. We told each other all about our lives before we came to Baxter, though Bernard had so much more to tell being an older guy at forty-eight. I guess it helped that we both liked country music and the Boston Red Sox, but there was more to it. Bernard was genuine and really cared about the park and the people he worked with. It just so happened that I was able to work with him on a daily basis. You kind of get to know someone fairly well in that situation. Bernard was old school and didn't just take to anyone. If you were a slacker and shirked your duties, chiseled overtime pay, or didn't put in a full-day's work—you can be sure Bernard would not be impressed and would call you out on it.

So, when Bernard invited me to his camp for break time one day, it was a surprise to me. We usually took a break sometime between 9:30 and 10 in the morning. Most times, we just drank some water and rested where we were for 10 or 15 minutes. Other times, we would go to our respective camps for a snack. This day was different. "Well, Steve, why'nt we go on up to the camp and see if Alice has the kettle on?" There you have it. Bernard thought enough of me to invite me up to his camp for break. So, we hopped into Bernard's truck and drove the ¼ mile to his camp. Bernard's wife, Alice, had the kettle on all right. Bernard and I sat at the table and he gestured toward a Lazy Susan-type fixture in the center.

"Here, pick one or two," he said as he spun it around. It must have held some 14 varieties of Little Debbie snacks. I hadn't known there were that many at the local IGA grocery store. As the table version Lazy-Susan device slowed to a stop, I grabbed a couple snacks. My life-long addiction to Little Debbies started that day and it was all Bernard's fault. Little Debbies are tasty and inexpensive and for a ranger on a budget, they were perfect. At the Millincoket IGA, Little Debbies were half the price of a similar Hostess item. Bernard and Alice doled out Little Debbies quite often at Togue Pond. Sometimes Bernard would bring along an extra stash of Debbies if we were going to be too far away to run back to his camp for break.

Working at Baxter Park is different than working in a factory or an office building. In the average workplace, workers take break alone or in a company-owned break room. At Baxter, unless you were working solo at a backcountry campground, you'd often have break either at your co-worker's camp or they'd be at your camp. Our camps were our homes. Often times, people like Bob Howes and his wife Jeanne invited other rangers over for dinner just because. Your co-workers really are your friends at Baxter.

Most of the seasonal rangers were on a tight budget. So, every so often, Dave and I would combine forces and see what we could whip up in the pantry. We'd invite other rangers over, too, for a change of scenery. Lester Kenway, the trail crew leader, was able to attend many of our potluck suppers. Lester knew his trails—knew where and how to place water bars for erosion control, stone steps up the steeper slopes and bridges over the wet areas. He would train his new crew every spring. For the most part, his trail crew was from the Student Conservation Association or SCA. These were dedicated college students who worked hard for room and board and a small stipend. I was able to work and train with several trail crews when it came to hiker rescues and first aid training. Lester also provided lively entertainment for Dave and me. He usually "earned" his meal with a little comic relief. His spot-on imitation of Maine folk humorist, Tim Sample, was a favorite of ours. It wasn't long before we all put the exaggerated Maine accent to use.

The summer of 1986 at Baxter was really just a long spring. It never really got hot and the northwest wind blew hard across Upper Togue Pond so often that white caps were visible all the time. Sometimes the wind was fierce enough that it created two-foot waves that crashed violently on the banks below Dave's camp. The spray would actually come through his porch screen and into his camp if he left his main door open. With weather like this, we sometimes craved a little more of a meal than a can of spaghettios. That's when we would combine forces and create a new pantry invention. One such pantry combination became a classic around Togue Pond.

Now, I don't remember all the ingredients or how much of each that we used, but Dave and I whipped up the meatiest, chunkiest, spiciest and most flavorable chile you can imagine. It was christened "Chile-Con-Tardiffimo" after Dave's last name because we concocted it at Dave's camp. The chile pretty much contained a can of everything we had in our pantries and a dash of every spice we could lay our hands on. Dave, being the astute cook he was, added a little dumpling action with a handy box of Jiffy mix.

Some chilies are sweet. Some are so hot and spicy you can barely eat them. Ours was just the right blend of haphazard ingredients thrown together and cooked slow and low. Between the two of us, we ate the equivalent of a 4-quart saucepan. It went down smooth. It was just that "Chile-Con-Tardiffimo" had after effects, or should I say, aftershocks. The full power of "Chili-Con-Tardiffimo" didn't kick in until a few hours later. Indigestion and heartburn are mild words to describe the post-chili eating evening. Suffice it to say this—there was a well-worn path to the outhouse from the direction of both our camps. No ranger ever attempted to concoct "Chili-con-Tardiffimo" ever again.

Not long after the "Chile-Con-Tardiffimo Colonostomy," (as it later became known) I was working alone cleaning debris from the Togue Pond area. Bernard was the duty ranger that day. Every 4th or 5th week, he would spend the day traveling the park roads and visiting other rangers at campgrounds and gatehouse. His main duty was to retrieve the receipts and cash and deliver them to park headquarters. It really was an all-day affair as Baxter Park covers lots of territory. Its small perimeter road only allows for a speed limit of 20 mph. A duty ranger could end up traveling at least 70 miles on narrow dirt roads with side trips to campgrounds, not to mention the 40 or 50 miles to return via state roads. With all the stops to pick up money and receipts, a visit and coffee with each ranger and gatehouse attendant, a duty ranger's day was long indeed. Somehow, I still thought it was a play day for the duty ranger. As duty ranger, you were able to see the whole park, maybe see a moose or bear, visit with all the other rangers and usually get a break from the tourist crowds.

The debris being removed was brush, wood and other biodegradable stuff that had been allowed to collect in the Togue Pond area by the various past private owners of Togue Pond. Not only was the shoreline reclamation in the works, but also a general "de-civilizing" the Togue Pond area was in order. Baxter Park's plan was to bring Togue Pond back to a condition that looked natural with no man-made scars on the land. This held true of many of the buildings. While I was there, several camps were torn down and removed. Today, there are but two buildings left—the old block building, which now houses a visitor center and another building a few feet away. This building was new in 1986 and has been refurbished and may be used to house VIP's. If I remember correctly, eleven or twelve buildings were either torn down or moved to another park location over the years. Bernard's camp, Dave's camp, and my camp—they're all gone. Unless you knew the area beforehand, you'd never know a camp existed there.

Anyway, I loaded up my park-issued GMC 3500 Sierra dump truck with debris. Yes, I had one of only two ranger dump trucks in the park. It wasn't as snappy as Greg's four-wheel drive ranger truck at Roaring Brook campground, but it made life easy when getting rid of debris, dirt or bark mulch. Because the debris was all-natural, we could dump it in special areas in the park. Since it wasn't trash or garbage-type stuff, it wouldn't hurt the environment or attract critters looking for a man-made food source. On my way back from a dump run that day, I had one of the nicer experiences ever as a ranger. The Roaring Brook road makes a sharp bend to the right just as you leave the Togue Pond gatehouse. And, on your left there is a water flowage and a beautiful view of Katahdin. Once in a while, you might catch a glimpse of a moose feeding on the underwater plants. It had been a quiet day traffic-wise and I could see a vehicle parked along side the road near the flowage. Two people were standing outside of the car and watching a cow moose and her twins. Ranger or not, it was still exciting to see wildlife up close, so I stopped to look, too.

"MOTHER MOOSE AND TWINS AT TOGUE POND"

I didn't want to infringe on the park visitors' experience, but I noticed they were taking pictures of the moose with a rather boring and uninspired background. If they moved a little to their left, they'd have a nice picture of mama and babies with mighty Katahdin as a spectacular backdrop. I was maybe ten feet from them. Their backs were turned as they were watching the moose. I said something to the effect that it wasn't often that people get to see a mother moose and young this close to the road. No answer. No acknowledgement. Hmm. "If you move to your left about 20 yards, you'll get the mountain in the background and the moose in the foreground. It'd make a great picture for you." Nothing. They just kept taking pictures. They weren't even talking amongst themselves.

"Geez," I thought to myself. "So much for trying to be charming and helpful." As I was turning to go back to my truck, the woman turned my way and saw me. Her eyes lit up and she had a big beautiful smile. She tapped her companion (her husband, I learned later) on the shoulder. She started talking to me but I couldn't understand her at first. Then I realized both of them were hearing impaired. She explained that neither of them could hear at all and that only she was able to read lips. Her husband could not. As long as I faced her when I spoke, she could understand me. Slowly, I was able to understand her.

They had spent a week in Baxter and were on their way home and these were the only moose they had seen. Baxter moose can be that way. Some days you can see ten moose. Then you can go a whole week and not see a thing. She said that they had enjoyed their visit immensely, but for some reason I was the only ranger who had talked to them and had given them moose information and advice on picture taking. They couldn't believe the difference in picture quality when they used my suggestion. She asked many questions about moose and Baxter Park. She used sign language to relay what I said to her husband. They seemed like people who kept to themselves and that could explain why other rangers hadn't talked to them. Most rangers at Baxter love the public relations stuff with visitors. But, we also like to let folks alone to enjoy their wilderness stay. If visitors approach us and ask questions, we're more than happy to chat and help them out. However, we'd only approach them, say, at their campsite to remind them to keep their site clean, where they can get water—things like that. It's possible that some visitors will only talk briefly with at gatehouse ranger on the way in and maybe just once at the campground when they get their site. Unless a visitor is forthcoming, most rangers are reluctant to force their knowledge on them.

These two people were so moved by seeing the moose and having the moose life cycle explained to them by a ranger. They were literally moved to tears. They were so thankful. I couldn't quite understand the crying, but maybe they just felt happy that their trip was complete and they could go home and tell everyone that a ranger helped them with their moose picture. I took a picture of them with their camera. The three moose and Katahdin were behind them. If the picture came out, they have a beautiful keepsake memory of their visit. I, too, have a nice memory of helping to make someone's visit more enjoyable.

Earlier that spring, several truckloads of tree-length cedar logs had been delivered to Togue Pond. These logs were to be part of the shoreline reclamation and had to be sorted and de-barked before use. Cedar was used because it stands up to the elements very well. An untreated cedar pole in the ground may last 20-30 years before it starts to decay. We cut various lengths for post-and-rail fences that would designate parking areas and for posts and cross pieces for the lake shoreline. On the shoreline, we constructed terraces with the cedar logs to hold bark mulch and soil. Grass and trees were planted in the hopes that the shore would stop eroding and the natural vegetation would hold the soil in place.

Sorting, de-barking and cutting the logs to length was time consuming and usually required Bernard and me to join forces. Many times we'd make use of a cedar log's natural curve if it went with the contours of the shoreline section we were working on. In order to move these tree length logs by hand we used a tool that is the lumbermen's standby—a cant-dog. I'd never heard the term cant-dog until the day Bernard asked, "Hand over that cant-dog over there, will you, Steve?" I had no clue what I was supposed to hand over to Bernard. "Okay, Bernard. You got me. What's a cant-dog?" Bernard explained what a cant-dog is and what a cant-dog can and can't do.

Of course, I recognized the tool by its more modern name—the peavey. A cant-dog is a pole about four feet long with a sharp, stout point on the bottom. It has a hinged hook partway up from the pointed end. A man gets leverage on a log when the hook grabs the log and the point digs into the log as you lift on the pole. You can lift and turn a log as needed in this manner. Bernard and I moved many a log this way. Sometimes the logs couldn't be moved any other way except by brute strength—one guy lifting from either end. Now, if you've met Bernard, you know he's a pretty hefty man. I'd go as far to say that he's a bear of a man. At 48 years old, he could still easily lift twice what I could at twenty-two. It was all I could do just to keep up with him on tough jobs. Bernard was usually courteous enough to always lift the big end of the log.

One day I was having a little trouble with my end. Bernard had his end at waist-level and ready to move. Of course, Bernard saw fit to kid me about being a weak college boy still wet behind the ears. I was giving him an "old man" type of insult in return when all of a sudden, someone punched me in the eye and down I went. I never saw it coming. Sucker-punched for sure. My end of the log went flying and caught Bernard off balance, but he managed to keep his feet. I was still down, dazed and holding my eye. What the heck happened? There was nobody there but me and Bernard and he couldn't have delivered the blow from the far end of the 30-foot log.

It turns out that there was a nest of white-faced hornets in my end of the log and one or two decided to sting my eyelid for the trouble I was causing them. Bernard took a look at my eye that was starting to swell shut. My head felt like I'd been whacked with a baseball bat. I'd live, no doubt. It was just a painful reminder that not all cedar logs are created equal. Bernard suggested that we go up to his camp and see if Alice had a remedy for my wasp sting. Bernard thought it was all sort of comical once he knew I'd survive. "Well, Steve," he said with a smirk. "Better you than me." He laughed and guffawed all the way to his camp. He laughed and guffawed the entire time Alice doctored my swollen eye. I would remember that one (and so would Bernard) before the week was over.

Now, in the mid-1980's, the Togue Pond gatehouse was situated about 200 yards closer to the actual gate than it is today. Today, the gatehouse is located right where the road forks—the right fork to Roaring Brook campground and a dead end and the left fork is the perimeter road leading around the park to exit at the Mattagamon gate in the north end. Katahdin was and still is the most popular destination for Baxter Park hikers. Roaring Brook campground is the favored spot for most hikers to start their Katahdin climb. But there are only so many parking spaces (maybe 100) and once the Roaring Brook parking lot is full, that's it—no more vehicles were allowed in. The hikers were directed to take the left fork that leads to the not-so-popular west side trails. Most folks did as the Togue Pong gate rangers instructed them.

Others (and there were many) figured they were out of sight of the gate rangers and they'd do what they wanted. They would go to Roaring Brook anyway, park off the road, trample the vegetation, and cause ruts and erosion. Preservation first and recreation second is Baxter's creed. Park managers needed a stopgap of some sort. That's when I was given the job of "fork-in-the-road ranger". My only duty was to block the right fork with my dump truck and move it only for those leaving Roaring Brook or those with a valid camping permit for that side of the park. Day users who tried to sneak in to Roaring Brook were stymied.

Still, many tried to bluff their way by me. Some tried to bribe me with money. One lady actually offered some "adult fun" once her hike was done if I let her and her friends pass. When these tactics failed, they'd swear and cuss at me before they tromped on their gas pedals so hard that they'd sling gravel and dust everywhere. Even with a well-thought out explanation as to why it was important not to overcrowd certain areas of the park, many people were just angry and unreasonable. Sometimes I'd have to call Bob in when some folks got out of hand. By noontime or so, the hiking rush would be over and I could return to my regular duties.

That Sunday of the same week of my hornet attack, I was pulling fork-in-the-road ranger duty. Bernard decided he'd do some work around the cedar log pile by himself. He needed to hitch the big flatbed trailer to the big dump truck so he could ferry some logs over to the worksite. I met up with him sometime after lunch and noticed his hand was wrapped in gauze. It looked like he was wearing a white boxing glove. Hmm, more than just a splinter I was sure. But, Bernard wasn't forthcoming with an explanation so I prodded him a little. "So, Bernard, what'd you do this morning while I was out at the checkpoint holding off the crowds?"

"Oh, nothing too much. Prob'ly use a hand hitching up the flatbed to the dump truck." Bernard was evasive.

"Nothing much, huh, Bernard? So what's with the white boxing glove?" This ought to be interesting.

"Well, I was trying to hitch up the flatbed and I had a hold of the tongue. It rolled a little too far and too fast and pinched my hand between the hitch and that boulder right there," he answered, pointing with his good hand. Bernard knew I had him. Of course, I couldn't help but laugh a little. My eye wasn't swollen anymore, but it was still sore. And, I remembered how cheery Bernard was about my hornet misfortune earlier in the week. I just had to say it. "Well, Bernard, better you than me."

CHAPTER 8

ODDS AND ENDS

When you live and work in a place such as Baxter State Park, one thing is for certain—you never know what the coming day (or night) will bring. Nothing is predictable. Nothing is guaranteed. The weather can change instantly from good to bad or bad to good. You may start the day with both feet solidly on the ground yet end that same day flying high over Katahdin. You might meet the nicest park visitor right after breakfast and by suppertime find yourself in the midst of a squabble with a crowd of unruly drunks in the day use area. One minute you can be driven crazy by the hoards of blackflies and you wish you were someplace else, and the next minute you might be privy to the sight of a mother moose nurturing her young.

In the three-plus seasons that I spent at Baxter (so brief compared to fellow rangers who have been there as many as 35+ years), I don't recall every being bored. There might not have been daily adventures, but there was always something new to see and always someone new to meet. And as you've seen over the previous pages, some of the folks could become your friends and some your enemies.

Now, before I get too far ahead of myself, I should try to explain how things were during my days at Baxter. Part of my compensation as a roadside field ranger was the use of a park vehicle and a camp to live in during the season. And in all fairness, the Park could dictate when and where I drove the truck and who could come along with me. The same held true for the use of the camp. Though my camp was not insulated and lacked indoor plumbing (unlike most other ranger camps), it was still considered decent shelter from the weather and bugs. At that time, there were unwritten park policies that forbid single rangers from having overnight guests of the opposite sex. Of course, these policies did not include visiting family members. It simply meant that a young, unattached ranger (such as I was) could not have an unrelated female guest spend the night. And it didn't matter whether she was a love interest or not. Even a platonic friend of the opposite sex was not allowed. Of course, I was in complete disagreement with these unwritten and mostly unspoken policies and proceeded to casually ignore them. Looking back, I can understand why these policies might have been needed, but at the time, I was young, impetuous and stubborn—three factors that can get a guy into trouble quickly as you've seen.

Now, during my first season at Baxter, I was truly an unattached ranger. No girlfriend, no wife and no significant other. But rangering in a wilderness area can be a lonely life if you know what I mean. So when opportunities presented themselves, I made the most of them, regardless of a "policy" that seemed to infringe on my rights as a human being living free on the earth. I regarded this "no overnight guests of the opposite sex" policy much the same as the length of hair policy the park had. It's not like I wore my hair long in a ponytail (I never had much hair to begin with), but Bob Howes had to constantly remind me to keep my hair no longer than my uniform collar. My main objection to the hair policy was that it was costly. There wasn't much hair growing on the top of my head, but the rest grew just fine. In order to keep Bob happy and maintain proper ranger presentation, I had to visit the barber once every few weeks. What, with the forty-mile roundtrip to Millinocket and the cost of the barber, I was running low on funds that summer—not including my shower donations to Bob's son.

"AUTHOR ON SENTINEL MT.
WITH KATAHDIN AND THE OWL BEHIND"

Most of the "opportunities" for meeting the opposite sex while at Baxter were not aggressively sought by me—they just kind of happened. Take for instance the way I ended up meeting a woman that we'll just refer to as Sheila the Surfer Girl. As you've been able to ascertain from previous chapters, I spent most days at Baxter either working hard or hiking far and wide. I really did try to be proper and represent Baxter Park in a professional and decent manner. At the same time, however, I wasn't above going a little bit out of my way to ingratiate myself with a stunningly beautiful (and hopefully single) woman.

Togue Pond was good to me. Those blustery west winds (I cursed them many times) that kicked up two-foot waves and sent spray through Dave Tardiff's front door also kept biting insects at bay and brought Sheila the Surfer Girl to my shore. I was eating lunch on my screened-in porch and minding my own business. It was one of those very windy but warmer days. I noticed a bright pink triangle float by the high lake bank at a fairly quick clip. The big white pines that lined the lake bank obstructed most of my view. It looked like the top of a sailboat, though I hadn't seen much sailing activity on either Upper or Lower Togue Pond all summer. I decided to investigate further. So, with fluffernutter in hand, I strolled to the top of the bank. From that vantage point, I spied a very shapely and tanned young woman wearing a very revealing bikini. She was windsurfing on a bright pink sailboard. Both sail and board were the brightest pink I'd ever seen. With mighty Katahdin as a backdrop, this young ranger beheld one beautiful sight. This was definitely better than the mama moose charge or even Mr. Black Bear grabbing at bread slices from a truck's hood.

The young woman was not far offshore and she spotted me watching her. She maneuvered her sailboard over to where I stood, introduced herself and immediately started to ask questions about Baxter Park. Maybe it was the ranger uniform. Dutiful ranger that I was, I answered her questions between bites and swallows of my fluffernutter. Of course, it was a tad difficult concentrating on ranger professionalism as Sheila had the looks and smile of a top fashion model. Yet, she was so down to earth. It turned out that she was camping at Katahdin Stream campground for several days. I casually mentioned the campfire program that I presented on Saturday nights and hoped that she'd attend. She agreed to come listen to my program if I agreed to meet her at the end of my workday so she could teach me how to windsurf. I'm sure I got the better end of that deal.

Bernard could tell that I was a little antsy during the long afternoon. I didn't bother to tell him about Sheila. He'd have given me the business for sure. Besides, he might have been duty-bound to remind me of the unwritten "policy". Long about 4:30 p.m., I met Sheila on the Togue

Pond shoreline in front of the camps. I was now out of uniform and in my cut-offs. She'd been on the lake all afternoon, but she looked like she'd just stepped out of a salon. I spent a very pleasant late afternoon with a lovely and intelligent woman. I never did get the hang of windsurfing. There were too many distractions.

Sheila attended that Saturday's campfire program. Through our windsurfing conversation, she had learned that I played the guitar and that I often joined Katahdin Stream Campground Ranger Eric Merry at the program's end. He played guitar, too and sounded much better than I could ever hope to. Sheila invited me to her campsite after the program to play and sing. My private concert wasn't all that great, but she thought I played fine. At least the conversation was entertaining. Sheila was from California. I should have figured that one out. I could have easily fallen for that girl, but after that night, I never saw or heard from her again. It just goes to show how a well-timed fluffernutter lunch on your camp porch can lead to beautiful woman when you live on Togue Pond.

Most days were routine once the height of the tourist season arrived. I'd awaken to the tinny clanging of my Big Ben alarm clock at 6:45 a.m. Some days started much earlier if a sneaky mosquito slipped into my camp and decided to torment me. Camping at Togue Pond was not allowed, but day use was heavy. Bernard, Bob, and I, along with many volunteers, had constructed a nice beach and picnic area as part of the shoreline reclamation. People actually had a beautiful place to swim and picnic where none had previously existed. Most of day users were from the Millinocket area, though some of them were campers from within the park. Togue Pond Beach was used heavily during the warm weather. Part of my routine day was spent cleaning and re-supplying the public outhouses, cleaning the campfire pits at the picnic sites, and removing the surprising amount of litter left on the beach. The remainder of my day was spent on the many other projects I was involved in at Togue Pond.

But every now and then, something out of the ordinary would occur. One day in late May, there was a major forest fire in nearby New Brunswick, Canada—though we were unaware of that at the time. The weather pattern blew the smoke over most of northern Maine and it seemed as if there was a forest fire somewhere in Baxter Park—and very near Togue Pond. I had to meet with Chief Ranger Chris Drew and the two of us investigated. We each donned an Indian tank (water tanks we carried on our backs), carried a Pulaski (a cross between a pick and an adz) in one hand and a shovel in the other, and set off down a nearby tote road. We searched for quite some time but to no avail. There was no fire. After we'd pronged around for an hour or so in the heat carrying 40 pounds of sloshing water and awkward hand tools, we were notified that the heavy smoke was most likely from our neighbors in New Brunswick. Better safe than sorry.

Many days I'd be performing a mundane task within eyesight of the road and folks would drive up and ask me where they could fine a nice place to picnic. Of course, I'd direct them to Togue Pond's new beach and picnic area that *I* had just built. I would neglect to mention Bob or Bernard's assistance for some reason. And sometimes, the people found the picnic area so relaxing and beautiful that they'd come back to invite me for lunch or supper. Trust me when I say that most park visitors eat better than most single rangers. I enjoyed many a steak dinner with all the fixings at Togue Pond courtesy of friendly park visitors.

There were many instances when tourists were glad to see a ranger. Once, while I was attending a wilderness/first-aid training session at Roaring Brook campground, a visitor interrupted the class. He was a little panicky and for good reason. He needed help in getting his car unstuck. He had accidentally driven his car over a barrier log and the front end of his car hung precariously over Roaring Brook. His vacation looked to be over before it started. However, with the help of Lester Kenway's trail crew, we were able save his car and Roaring Brook. We also saved him the steep price he would have had to cough up for a tow truck operator's appearance.

One thing I learned quickly while at Baxter was that most park visitors came to Baxter for much the same reasons that we rangers loved working there. The rugged country, wildlife and solitude really do help to soothe the soul. Every now and then, folks come for other reasons. One evening well after dark when the day use area closed to visitors, Dave Tardiff and I saw what we thought was an illegal camper at Togue Pond. We saw this same car being driven back and forth along the Togue Pond. The driver would go up toward the beach area, stop and dim the lights. After several minutes, the driver illuminated his headlights and drove back down toward our end, stopped and dimmed his headlights again. It seemed as if the driver was looking for a secluded place to park or camp. Dave and I decided to investigate—mainly for the fact that Togue Pond was day use only.

Since we were off-duty, we had to throw on our ranger uniforms before we approached the driver. Dave went up to the passenger side though the driver was alone. I tapped on the driver's partially rolled down window and asked him if he was lost.

"No, I'm fine, thank you." And with that, he put his car in drive and went on his merry way back toward Togue Pond beach. We hadn't even reminded him that the park gate was closed and that Togue Pond was a day use area only. Dave and I quick-stepped it to the beach and re-confronted the man. This time we were a little more cautious and a little more forceful in our manner. We asked him what he was doing. He was acting very shifty and seemed to be hiding something from us. We asked him several times why he was driving back and forth along an area closed to night traffic because he would give a vague answer or none at all. Dave and I were becoming very suspicious.

Finally, the man claimed that he was out studying bats. "Do you have a study permit issued by Baxter Park, sir?" I asked him.

"No, I don't," he answered as he slowly reached into his shirt with his right hand in what seemed to be a deceptive manner. I thought for sure that he was going for a gun or a knife, as his behavior had been very erratic for a scientist. I hoped Dave was alert and would be able to identify the guy who killed me. The driver claimed he was just pulling out his "bat detector", though it didn't like much more than a chunk of wood to me. I think this guy could tell Dave and I were rookies and was playing around with our youthful ranger imaginations. We decided that we'd let him detect bats as long as he steered clear of Bob and Bernard's camps. To this day, over twenty years later, I carry a steel pipe in my pickup just because that batman guy freaked me out. I've never used that pipe in self-defense, but it has surely come in handy for extra leverage when loosening lug bolts on a flat tire.

Since I lived at Togue Pond, I was able to assist other rangers quite readily on either side of Katahdin. Being able to respond to both sides of the mountain, I was often called upon to lend a hand in minor rescues. One day while I was staining my camp that invisible brown color, Brian Johnston, the Abol Campground ranger called me in to help in a litter carry. A woman had broken her ankle on the Abol Slide trail. A litter carry is difficult enough over flat ground, but it's almost impossible on the lower reaches of the Abol Slide in high summer. The alders, brush and boulders trip, poke and grab at you as you stumble down the trail when you're hiking alone. Imagine this when you're now the equivalent of three persons wide and carrying a helpless individual in an oblong litter. It didn't help that in this case, the woman was heavier than most. And even though we were on the west side of Katahdin—far from our friend Pamola—he still let it rip with a violent thunderstorm just as we reached the injured woman. The thunder crashed so loudly that it seemed as if it were right on top of our heads. Of course, a deluge ensued. It was a tough slog bringing that woman down off the mountain.

Many people that I'd known previous to my ranger career made it a point to visit while I was stationed at Togue Pond. My parents and friends came up regularly to stay several days at a time. I even received a surprise from my high school biology teacher and her husband. She and her husband usually summered on a lake in Downeast Maine and decided to come on up to Baxter where her former student worked. We had kept in touch through my college years because of our Maine connection. She said I'd done her biology class and the high school proud. One of the more surprising visits was from Bernard. It was not so surprising that he'd visit as his camp was only 500 yards away and I worked with him everyday. What made this visit surprising was because of what he brought with him. Bernard had found a kitten deep in the park near one of the campgrounds. Campers told him that there had been more than one kitten, but this one was the only survivor. He surmised that coyotes got the others. Someone had dropped off a litter of kittens in the wilds of Baxter—someone who was stupid and cruel no doubt.

Bernard figured I'd like to keep her since I was one of only two or three rangers who actually lived *outside* the boundaries of Baxter Park. Domestic pets are not allowed inside the park. At first, I was reluctant to take on the responsibilities of a pet. I kind of liked not having anyone or anything to answer to at my camp. I changed my mind when Bernard suggested that we'd have no choice but to bring her into town to the animal shelter. If she weren't adopted promptly, the animal shelter folks would be forced to euthanize her. So, I named the little kitten Butch. Why, you may ask? Well, she was nothing but a mischief-maker and I had always thought the name Butch and mischief were one and the same. Butch returned every year with me to my ranger camp on Togue Pond. It was good to have company. Butch did a good job lessening the mice population in my camp. She also did a good job lessening the amount of my sleep time while she made mischief at all hours of the night. She was one of the best friends that I made while I Baxter. She's not forgotten.

Some aspects of our ranger training could be very intense, while others were boring. The training for forest fire fighting was always a little fun. Sometimes the Park would go all out and hire a helicopter and pilot. Rangers would get flown in and dropped off in the wilderness at a mock fire site to practice our skills. Once, we were treated to a helicopter pilot who had flown combat missions in Vietnam. He gave us a ride over Togue Pond that I'll never forget. As he brought me, Greg and another ranger back from the mock fire site, the pilot skirted the treetops, just clearing Bob Howes' camp and Togue Pond gate. My bear dog-wrestling ranger buddy, Greg, challenged the pilot to give us the type of ride the pilot experienced in Vietnam. Well, the pilot wasn't afraid to showcase his flying skills and he obliged. Just as we cleared the trees on at the edge of Togue Pond, the pilot dropped that helicopter down so fast we didn't have time to blink. We skimmed along the surface of Togue Pond and just before it seemed we would crash into the trees on the far shore, the pilot lifted us up just as fast to clear the trees. All I really remember was the deep blue water outside the bubble windshield looking very close. Fire training.

Another flight I experienced over the northern Maine woods would be hard to pull off today post 9/11. I was a Baxter State Park ranger. But in the vicinity of Baxter Park, there were forestry rangers and game wardens. I became friendly with one of the local forestry rangers and I casually mentioned how I loved flying and seeing the countryside. He told me about how the State of Maine Forestry Service had some sort of deal whipped up with local pilots at small airports throughout Maine. During bouts of dry weather, the pilots were expected to make twice daily flights looking for possible forest fires. They'd run flight patterns crisscrossing Maine's wildest country. My forestry ranger friend said that any forestry ranger was eligible to fly for free with these pilots anytime. He said that all I needed was a forestry ranger's shirt and hat, which he supplied. I could go right into the Millinocket airport, tell the pilot that I was directed to fly with him as part of my training, and voila—I'd get a free flying tour over the northern Maine woods.

So, with my borrowed (and slightly large) forestry uniform and a little bravado, I was able to fly all over northeastern Maine from Millinocket to Danforth to Topsfield and Grand Lake Stream. Quite a ride, and costing me not a cent. But I paid for my sneakiness, as we had to land during a violent thunderstorm back in Millinocket. I really thought we were going to crash. It probably would have served me right for impersonating another ranger type. I didn't think we were in Pamola's jurisdiction, but it sure looked like one of his storms. Trust me when I say that I was quivering in my seat as the pilot threaded his way through that thunderstorm to land on the Millinocket runway. I couldn't see a thing out of the windshield. The rain was so heavy it was as if we were actually underwater. That pilot earned his pay that afternoon as far as I'm concerned.

Part of my job as ranger at Togue Pond was to assist other rangers throughout the park when they needed help. Since I didn't have any campers to worry about, I was usually free to go and help. Many times I lent a hand to Albert Rickards, the maintenance ranger. "Big Al," as I called him, was my age and had started at Baxter the same year I had. Big Al didn't worry about campers, hikers or moose. His job was to build or repair park buildings—ranger camps, lean-tos, outhouses, etc. He was hired for his carpentry skills. Big Al could manufacture an outhouse that was luxurious enough to live in. But he had no clue when it came to hiking or carrying supplies in a backpack.

One week I was volunteered by Bernard to go on a "working" vacation at Chimney Pond campground. I was to assist Big Al and Esther Hendrickson, the Chimney Pond campground ranger, replace the roof on the ranger station. Heavy supplies such as the shingles, tarpaper, nails and lumber had been brought up the past winter. Bob, Bernard and other year-round rangers had brought these up via snow sled. All that Big Al and I had to do was hike the 3.3 miles to Chimney Pond, work a few days and return. I had my backpack ready. I'd packed a few days' changes of clothes and food for two or three days—light stuff such as oatmeal, pop-tarts, dried noodles and a couple of snacks. Lightweight—twenty-five pounds maximum. That Big Al was a novice hiker there is no doubt. But he must have been a very hungry boy, too. I swear that his pack had fourteen cans of Chunky soup, five cans of tuna fish, three loves of bread, and an assortment of Hostess products (Big Al didn't go for Little Debbie snacks). He had enough food in his pack to last thirty-five days in the woods. Heavyweight—eighty-five pounds minimum. Needless to say that Big Al's behind was dragging long before we reached Chimney Pond's 2914' elevation. You'd have to check with Esther to be sure, but I don't recall Big Al being all that helpful that afternoon on the ranger station's roof.

Sometimes, if a campground ranger needed extra time off or it was on either end of their assistant's season, I would fill in at various campgrounds. I covered all the southern end campgrounds at one time or another during my days at Baxter—Abol, Katahdin Stream, Roaring Brook and Chimney Pond. While covering for Esther at Chimney Pond, I ran into a nice group of people that quickly turned mean. I even had to call Bob on the park radio for voice backup. I had learned from my Maine state senators encounter the previous season.

As the day nears its end, most campers who have a site at Chimney Pond will arrive and register at the ranger station. One such group of six or seven individuals was all excited about its planned trip over Katahdin the next day. The group was also flying high as they'd just seen a moose as they entered the campground. The group had a few questions that I answered and then I reminded them that they were in a backcountry campground. They would need to take precautions with their foodstuffs and toiletries by hanging them in packs from the bear line set up for campers.

"Oh, we won't have much left after supper for bears," they explained. "We're having steaks and baked potatoes." For a moment, a vision of juicy steaks and buttery potatoes clouded my thinking. Then I realized that my camper friends were planning on cooking these steaks and potatoes over an open fire—a definite no-no at backcountry sites in Baxter Park. I inquired about their cooking methods. "We brought a charcoal grill!"

"Charcoal and all?" I asked, knowing the obvious answer.

"Yes, and five pounds of potatoes. Oh, it's gonna be a great meal, cooked outside way up here!" Their exuberance was understandable, but I was going to have to squash it.

"AUTHOR AND FAMILY AT CHIMNEY POND"

"Folks, open fires are not allowed in backcountry sites like Chimney and charcoal fires are considered open fires. We're too remote up here to allow open fires that may get away and start the forest on fire. Sorry." I knew my steak dinner was history, but I didn't expect their vicious reaction.

"Whaddya mean—it's not allowed? We called before we left home and the lady at headquarters said we could bring the grill and charcoal!" I was sure they had misunderstood the person at headquarters. Every Baxter employee, especially those employees who deal with the public, knows the rules and regulations of the park. Fire safety is a big one. I told the group that very thing. They went ballistic right there in the Chimney Pond ranger's office. It wasn't pretty.

"We just 'bleeping' hiked three and a half miles with eight T-bones packed in ice, five pounds of potatoes, our grill and twenty-five pounds of charcoal! And you're telling us we can't even 'bleeping' cook it now?" "Bleeping" was not the word they used. I'm sure you can fill in the blank. Yup, that's the word they used.

"You can cook your meal—but just not on any type of open fire. In a frying pan over a Coleman stove or something like that—that's okay. But not on a wood or charcoal fire. It's much too dangerous as far as potential forest fires," I replied. At this point, some of the group led the angriest of the bunch outside. Another of the group stayed inside and tried to reason with me. I radioed headquarters and asked the reservations clerk who had spoken to the group if she recalled the conversation. She did. She also recalled that she distinctly told the caller that charcoal grills were allowed in front country sites only. She suggested that the caller misunderstood her. The person who had stayed behind in the office with me heard her comments. He apologized to me for his group's outburst. He turned and stepped outside to speak to his friends. I figured the matter was closed and all was well. It wasn't but two minutes later that the angriest group member came storming back in even more irate than before.

"You're a 'bleeping bleephole,' Mister!" he hollered at me. "What the 'bleep'! You're gonna ruin our 'bleeping' trip, man!" I wasn't about to listen to anymore of that. And I knew myself well enough to know that I could easily get drawn into a tit-for-tat argument with this fellow. I promptly radioed Bob and luckily he answered right away.

"Bob, did you happen to catch any of that radio traffic earlier about using charcoal grills at Chimney?"

"Yeah, Steve, I did. What's up?"

"Well, Bob, I've got one of the individuals from the group standing right here with me and he's a little steamed. He's not taking "no" for an answer and he's becoming a little more verbally abusive towards me than I care to hear." Bob reiterated the backcountry rules and regulations and the penalties if one should ignore them and specifically told my irate camper to watch his mouth. All right, Bob!

"Thanks a lot, Bob. Chimney clear."

"Okay, Steve. Five-three clear." The radio was silent. I sternly looked the fellow in the eye and said, "You've heard it, sir. From me, from headquarters and now from the District Ranger. It's even written in that pamphlet that you're holding. I'm sorry. No charcoal fires." The guy left without a word. The screen door had hardly slammed shut when he stomped back in.

"Oh, by the way—we were going to invite you to share a steak and potato with us. Now we're not. Hope you like your cup of soup." Then he left—for good. Such can be the life of a hungry ranger.

CHAPTER 9

THE END GAME

It wasn't long before I met my first wife during the off-season. We married and tried to make a go of it. Our home was in Connecticut. My ranger job was in northern Maine. She'd come up with my young stepsons, Tom and Bob, for the summer months, but May, June, September and October we would be apart save for bi-weekly visits home on my days off. I would return to Connecticut every fall and work wherever I could to sustain us until it was time for me to return to Baxter in early May. I worked with the landscaping company that had helped put me through college and the local car wash to make ends meet while my wife worked at a local food processing plant. This sort of worked the first two years, but at the start of my last season at Baxter, my wife was pregnant with our firstborn, Amie. My wife needed me at home. I would have to give up my lifelong dream. Baxter Park was almost like the other woman. I wanted both. We had tried hard to move to Maine and be closer to the park, but things didn't go our way. I gave my notice to Bernard one day in late May. We were working on more picnic sites at Togue Pond. By this time, Bernard and I were good friends and sometimes I thought of him as an extra father. I remember that he looked a little surprised at first, but Bernard knew it all along.

"Well, Steve, I kinda figured you'd be leaving us once you got married and all. And when you came back this spring as an "expecting" daddy—I'm surprised you even came back at all. You'll have to write out a formal written resignation and hand it in. Guess we'll kinda miss you around here." I left Baxter Park on June 3, 1989. It was one of the hardest things I had ever had to do. But it was the right thing to do. A man's wife and children have to come first.

Having a newborn baby helped to ease my Baxter Park withdrawal, but it was still almost two years before I finally got over the Park and my rangering career. It was difficult to go from an outdoorsy, no time clock type of job to a highly controlled factory job. And, I didn't want to ranger anywhere else. In my mind, any park other than Baxter was a step down. There were no parks wild enough in southern New England. Someone said that all good things must come to an end. I was just another in a long line of Baxter Park rangers. Katahdin's still there and the moose, bears, and other critters still roam the lands that Governor Baxter preserved for us.

I guess that it was fitting that on one of my last days as a Baxter State Park ranger I would see something beautiful. It was early morning and I was on the shoreline looking across Upper Togue at Katahdin. I was trying to drink in all that I could of this place that I had fallen in love with. I was leaving it and didn't know if or when I'd ever return. I knew that I'd never be a ranger here again. Unless you are fortunate enough to become a year-round ranger or live near enough to the Park that you can easily see your family, it is very difficult to return every year for six months of employment. It's hard to find work in the winter, and if you do, the winter job is hard to get again the following winter. It's a shame that things come down to money. Anyway, while I was trying to absorb all that I could of my adopted home, I saw a large bird soaring overhead. I couldn't believe my eyes. It was a bald eagle—the first I'd seen since I started at Baxter! It came low, right in front of me, maybe thirty yards offshore, and plucked a fish right out of Togue Pond! It was just like what you see on those wildlife shows on television. What a sight!

**"BALD EAGLE IN FLIGHT AFTER PLUCKING A FISH
FROM TOGUE POND"**

I said farewell to all my ranger friends and wished them well. By this time I owned a Ford 150 pickup truck and I packed it with my belongings along with Butch the cat and set out for Connecticut. Some of my ranger friends are retired now like Bernard. Some are still there, like Bob and Greg, carrying on the Baxter legacy. All of them have had ranger adventures and experiences that could fill three books the size of this one. Maybe when you next visit Baxter State Park, you'll run across a ranger. Ask him or her to share a Baxter story with you. There's so much more to tell.

**"AUTHOR, CENTER, WITH RANGERS GREG HAMER
AND SCOTT FISHER"**

THE END

Edwards Brothers Malloy
Thorofare, NJ USA
February 27, 2015